47

47

By Cliff McCrath

About the Author: Cliff McCrath

Cliff McCrath's long career as an NCAA men's soccer coach spanned 47 years and four universities. He co-founded Northwest Soccer Camp in 1972, now in its 47th year of operations, and he continues to coach U.S. international teams. Among his many awards and accomplishments:

- *U.S. Soccer's Lifetime Achievement Award*

- *12 Halls of Fame*

- *Seattle Sports Star of the Year*

- *Winner of the Bill Jeffrey Award for excellence in coaching*

- *597 collegiate game victories*

- *5 NCAA National Championships*

- *National Coach of the Year*

- *College coach, educator and administrator (49 years)*

- *Secretary-Editor, NCAA Soccer Rules Committee (40 years)*

- *Coach of the Year (30 times)*

- *National administrator for five years of all college soccer referees*

- *Creator and commissioner of two soccer collegiate conferences*

- *All American Athlete*

Author Cliff McCrath at the World University Games in Taiwan, 2017.

For KC, Stevie, Kieran and Sienna

Words -
my "Dad",
my Pal!,
my
Live Forever
plus 47 days!

"Cliffy"

Contents

PART TWO

PART THREE

Preface

A Little Help for My Friends

I first came to Seattle in 1970, hired by Seattle Pacific College (now University) to coach the men's soccer team. This was after more than a decade of coaching collegiate soccer in Illinois, Massachusetts and Michigan, a journey that began at Wheaton College in the 1950s.

Within a few years of coming to Seattle, I co-founded Northwest Soccer Camp in 1972. I put my heart into travelling the state with my 39-page pamphlet, running soccer clinics throughout Washington, teaching the fundamentals of soccer to a growing number of young recreational players. The parents recruited to coach their kids needed the basics, too, because soccer was new to most people in the Northwest at the time. In this way, I became a coach's coach.

While traveling to and from Seattle in the early days, I often passed a billboard on Pacific Highway South that read, "Will the last person leaving SEATTLE - *Turn out the lights*." Massive layoffs at Boeing devastated the Emerald City economically, resulting in tens of thousands of jobs lost. Seattle was then a rough and tumble port city, and the Tech Age was years away.

Growing up in Detroit, I was used to hard times, so it didn't daunt my optimism for soccer one bit. Good thing! Today, many of the parents, camp counselors and children who took part in Northwest Soccer Camp over the last 47 years are coaches of youth, high school and college soccer teams. More than 150 of my former collegiate players (including my son) are coaches now, too, and I'm honored by that.

Exactly 40 years after I received the NCAA National Coach of the Year Award in 1978, my son Steve McCrath won the same honor in 2018. He is the longtime head soccer coach for Barry University in Florida, winner of the 2018 NCAA Division II Men's Soccer National Championship! I am so very proud.

People tell me they have never coached, or have little experience coaching, and don't know where to begin. Well, I didn't start out as a soccer coach. In fact, I knew very little about the sport before I began playing it in college, so I was an unlikely candidate to become a future Hall of Fame soccer coach.

Yet, I had the joy of coaching men's college soccer teams for half a century. I continue to coach today, more than 60 years after my first coaching assignment, most recently for a U.S. Women's Team at the 2017 World University Games in Taipei. It was also my privilege to counsel generations of students and young married couples in the academic community. And, for the past decade, I've had the opportunity to speak to executives at companies such as Ford, Charles Schwab, and Nike, sharing strategies for coaching to excel with business leaders. Coaching transcends sport!

For some reason, people think I'm a funny guy, but the truth is, it would take a book to cover all the mistakes I've made. Perhaps this book should be called "Mission Edification." I like to build people up, and it's not just the person who has stumbled and is falling, because we all need shoring up from time to time.

This book contains 47 winning strategies, which are the guideposts and building blocks I use for Mission Edification. My hope is that these strategies continue to provide an uplifting source of strength and a launch pad for many coaches to come.

PART I

Chapter 1
Seattle ~ 1970

Winning Strategy:
Begin with love.

I looked at the dark-haired beauty with movie star lips now parted to issue some innocent command to the movers, putting our life's belongings into the house on the hill. I stepped out of the car, parked in the shadow of the moving truck and simply stared at my lovely wife, who I had not seen in a week.

She came by plane to Seattle with our two children, Stacey, 6, and Stevie, 2, while I drove from Michigan. As she turned on her heel toward the car, I took in at once the curve of her hips and the exquisite shape of her legs.

"Girlie, your skirt is too short," I teased, repeating the words of a Michigan matron at our previous college in Spring Arbor, Michigan.

I drew her to me kissing her on the lips. She blinked her pretty eyes at me in the soft Seattle light, Midge, my young wife. In the distance, a radio played as the movers lifted the heavier furniture from the truck into the house. She bit her lip and patted the back of the sofa. It was a long trip and what a shame the movers were there! I couldn't wait to be alone with her, but at that moment, with so much to do, I do believe love was the 16th thing on her mind.

The journey from Michigan by car was one of vast open road, punctuated by local radio announcers as I drove through small cities. Each broadcast tower brought a break from the silence as I sped through Indiana, Illinois, Iowa, Nebraska, Wyoming, Idaho and Oregon on my way to Washington. I had a boy's mind, full of adventure, excited to get to Seattle and my new coaching post at Seattle Pacific.

While the workers unloaded, and Midge guided them, I went to meet our new neighbor, asking her where I might find the nearest soccer field. This opening question met with a little scorn, (which seemed to linger afterwards). She said she had no idea what a soccer field was, but there was a play area down the hill near Interbay, a former garbage dump, about a half-mile away. Eager to see it, I hopped in the car and sped down the hill, pulling up next to what did resemble a soccer field. However, it was in soggy shape and might easily double as a garbage dump.

On the far side of the field, I watched a man in black stamping out boundary lines with his feet. I could not make out his face, so I waited near a tiny shack, home for tools and rakes and other equipment, until he made the turn and slowed. Then I introduced myself.

"I'm Cliff McCrath, the new soccer coach at SPC," I said (Seattle Pacific College in those days).

I took in his piercing gaze, straight nose and the rosy cheeks below his cap.

In heavy Irish brogue, he replied, "I'm Mihail O'Rean but most people know me as Mike Ryan."

I didn't know how lucky this meeting would prove to be.

Chapter 2
Coach B.

Winning Strategy:

Get Organized and Live a Proper Life.

There was no soccer to speak of in Detroit in the 1940s. Thus, there was no way of knowing in my younger years that I would one day live thousands of miles away in Seattle, coaching a team of underdogs to five national championships.

I was one of those stray dog kids, a wild-eyed whirling dervish from the Motor City. My early life was chaotic, bouncing around from home to home, and heck, they did not even play soccer in Detroit. At least no one knew it was played in the city where the Lions, Tigers and Red Wings were rulers of sport.

On the streets and back alleys, our game was Buicks versus Fords, a daily challenge between the Brewster Roosters and the Alfred Street Gang whereby we fought wars with hubcaps from "abandoned" cars. We hurled them like Frisbees at opponents, yelling, "Bop!" or "Crash!" or "Bang," or "Pow!" in the spirit of Captain Marvel, the cartoon hero of the day. A loud roar of "SHAZAAM" meant a direct hit.

Hanging out with a street gang landed me in front of a judge by the age of 15 and could have led to a life of miserable proportions. Luckily, that was not my fate. (More on this later.) Eventually a love for sports (and a girl, naturally) led me to Wheaton College and soccer.

In the 1950s, years before ESPN, there was not much American media coverage of soccer, even though "football" was played in Europe for well more than a century. The first NCAA soccer championship in the U.S. was not until 1959, and many college teams consisted of foreign players, though this was not the case for Wheaton's team.

When my college roommate talked me into turning out for the sport in 1955, I thought soccer was a game girls played at recess. Mike Easterling assured me it was not. He was a high-school All-American basketball player from Dallas who became a two-time All-American soccer player in college. "All-American" is an honorific title earned for being voted part of a hypothetical All America team, composed of the best players in a sport, for a specific season and for each position. In NCAA soccer, the National Soccer Coaches Association (now United Soccer Coaches) chooses the 11-member All-America team.

Coach B. took over as the men's soccer coach at Wheaton in 1951 and therefore he was my first coach. Not only did he run an organized and meticulous practice, his very life was a living, breathing definition of motivation. The man embodied habits, speech and ideals for living so far above reproach, his teams wanted to play their hearts out for him.

The center halfback position that I played on his team was a sweeper, tough and fast on the field. Prior to the first game (again, the first game of soccer I ever saw played, and was going to be playing in), I tried to research the sport at the library, but found just two books and very little information. Apparently, the jersey numbers traditionally indicated the positions on the field.

That bit of knowledge caused me some distress later because after telling everyone I knew to come to the game, Coach B. handed me jersey #47, (instead of #5). I was devastated, thinking that meant I wasn't playing. As it turned out, the team uniforms had not yet arrived, so the old football jerseys sufficed for the time being.

Coach B. rarely, if ever, raised his voice. People truly wondered if he ever sinned. His practices were clear as crystal and his style was to speak softly. He merely expressed his desires quietly, like asking for a napkin in a restaurant, and players stepped on each other trying to please him. However, his words carried a strength that transformed stray dogs, like me, into show dogs.

He was a quiet, thoughtful, somewhat mysterious man, Coach B., Dr. Robert Baptista. (We called his wife "Mama B.") He had coke-bottle thick glasses that made it difficult to determine the color and outline of his eyes. Somehow, he saw potential in me before I saw it in myself and encouraged me to stick with the sport a bit longer when I first wanted to quit. After my third season, in 1957, I was one of seven graduating seniors on the team that included three All American players.

Toward the end of the season, Coach B. gathered the team to inform us of his upcoming plans. We seven seniors huddled around him when he said, "Fellows, I'm leaving."

"What do you mean, leaving?" I asked.

Coach B. replied, "I have a sabbatical." (I had never heard the word.)

"Is it terminal?" I asked.

Laughter reigned, and as frequently occurred, my coach and teammates thought I was joking.

Coach B. said, "I'm going to get my PhD."

Then someone inadvertently offered a definition, and no one was any the wiser, except for me.

I jumped on the next question, "Who's going to coach next year?"

Coach B. didn't bat an eye; he looked at me and said, "You are!"

And he meant it. Thus, my first coaching job was for Wheaton in 1958, the fall season after I graduated. That was more than 60 years ago, but the lessons stick around. Young coaches ask me what they can do to motivate their players, and remembering Coach B., I tell them it's simple: Get organized and live a good life. It's the foundation of becoming a great coach.

Chapter 3
The Rookie Coach

Winning Strategy:
Arouse a fighting spirit!

I accepted the job coaching the Wheaton men's team because Coach B. told me I was going to be the coach. Moreover, when I got over the shock of being named the coach, it occurred to me there were only two things I really knew about how to approach this job. One, demanding respect was something I would never do because I grew up knowing respect was not something a person can demand.

Second, if indeed respect is the issue, it must be earned. No one will ever hear me ask for respect. What I do demand, though, is 100 percent of a player's effort, 100 percent of the time. Every returning player of mine knows that.

So, what does this mean?

It means if we all make a commitment to each other and dedicate ourselves to making every game the last thing we do on earth, then at least we can die with dignity and respect! If the opponent beats us, so be it, as long as the teams that take the field against us know they will never face a tougher challenge. I spoke those very words to my first team, on the eve of my first season as a coach.

Prior to my debut as a young soccer coach, a sportswriter for the *Chicago Sun-Times* predicted our team would have zero wins. Graduation and Coach B.'s departure did not bode well for the team now in the hands of a raw-boned, borderline lunatic who had never coached a day in his life (me). Prediction: Last place in the Midwestern Collegiate Soccer Conference!

Nonetheless, I started the season with these hopeful words, "Here's the way I see it guys, the pride of this program has always been our fighting spirit even when up against more talented players. We have always played with fury and pride."

Unfortunately, they simply didn't buy it. I was an inexperienced rookie coach and they knew it. As pre-season daily doubles progressed, what I saw on the practice field was indifference and defeat. The guys clowned around as if they didn't care. In this case, they believed the press clippings, which were obituaries of gloom.

Before the first game, I nearly threw in the towel. "Well, hear this," I said. "We have a choice! We can believe what they say and muddle through 'The Season That Wasn't,' and if this is your choice then I have a proposition for you. Today was the last practice of the year. We will not waste any more time practicing! It doesn't take any practice to lose!"

All eyes were upon me, transfixed. Breathing was suspended, but I wasn't done!

"You read the *Sun-Times*...A rookie coach and a team of leftovers without seven of their best starters, and a conference schedule that features players from all over the world. Who are you kidding? Hey, I'm an interim coach. I don't have to win one game!! Do you hear me?!"

I left the room and stood an eternity in the shower of the coach's locker room, not knowing what the outcome would be. However, the next day, I knew something was right when the "leftovers" defeated Indiana University 4-0. A victory over the conference champions was something our previous team of All Americans was never able to do.

I also knew something was right the following spring at the school's Annual Athletic Convocation held in Wheaton's chapel. The team and I were standing on stage behind the college president when he read a telegram from a PhD candidate studying at Indiana University, of all places.

The telegram read, "Congratulations! Great season! Great championship! Great team! Great coach!" It was signed, "Coach B.!"

Coach B. finished his PhD and returned the following year. In all, he coached the Wheaton men's soccer team for 16 seasons and in 1976 won the Honor Award, the highest recognition of the National Soccer Coaches Association of America. One of my greatest mentors, he lived a long and noble life until his death in 2015 at the age of 93.

The year I held the reins, while Coach B. was away on sabbatical, we defied the odds and beat the prediction of zero conference wins. Even though we played against several Big 10 schools (such as Indiana, Purdue, and Michigan State), we not only surpassed the prediction, Wheaton won the conference championship!

That year, I was named Coach of the Year for the first time, and it all began with the words that harnessed a fighting spirit in my team. In Greek, the word used to rouse a fighting spirit is *mimneskomai*. It means, "to remember," as if to conjure, to recall, to bring it to mind, to make it real and vivid.

Words are important tools in a coach's winning strategy, and they are most effective when players perceive choices. Reminding a team of something it already knows about itself, will make the players fight all the harder to make those words ring true.

Chapter 4
Coaching in the Tech Age

Winning Strategy:
Be a real time role model.

Coach B. represents an old-fashioned lesson on how to lead by example.

Without a doubt, he changed the direction and outcome of my life. Coaches

and leaders today have no less of a challenge. Yet some are losing focus on the

role model function in coaching, allowing technology to be the default change

agent.

When the answer to everything is Apple's trademarked slogan,

"There's an app for that," how do coaches proceed to teach players in real

time at a more lifelike pace? When kids arrive at the field as online experts,

wanting streaming videos, online schedules and social media communication,

this can appear to be an abject threat to many the seasoned coach.

I've been asked numerous times, "How do you keep up with the X/Y/Z Generation kids?"

My answer is, "I strap a keyboard to my forehead and head for the field. Then I wait for the kids to text me what they would like to do during practice!" Of course, I'm joking.

"Coaching," in the archaic sense of the word, meant to carry a student, as if by a coach. Coaching a team is to carry the team forward, preparing the players for success. Without a coach, the players are lost.

Prior to the tech era, there was a more methodical process to teach players the basic moves and technical skills such as dribbling and passing. Practice time on the ball is still necessary to develop the muscle memory needed for instant creativity and accuracy on the field.

Physical factors are beyond an online experience (at least for now). Examples of this include the weight of the pass, use of all areas of the foot, and soft receiving and preparation. Many technical elements must be practiced in the real world. For example, shooting and finishing require decisions about power versus finesse. Tackling is a combination of body position, patience, feints, committal and recovery, and so forth.

A coach guides players to move from offense to defense and make decisions to move the ball strategically. Physical components of practice, such as endurance, won't come passively looking at a screen. Certainly, the psychological factors of attitude and effort are results of experience in the real world, working together with the coach and teammates for a job well done.

That said, coaches should avoid clinging to the "same-old-same-old" of the bygone pre-tech coaching era. They must invest part of their preparation time on the method of presentation as well as the content of practice sessions. In brief, the "lead by example" principle is as simple as never trying to wing it with today's more sophisticated kids. Knowledge of the sport is essential as well as preparation to create the type of practice that will snap players to attention.

Add to this what I call the "Tiger Principle" from a Tiger Woods press conference gone wrong. What he – and all of us at one time or another – should have done is step to the mic and simply say: "I blew it! Are there any questions?"

It is important to build trust by letting players (or colleagues, if in business) see the human error and mistakes and owning the consequences. Yes, Gen Z kids spend seven to nine hours per day looking at a screen, yet they are also complex and optimistic, and will be the best-educated generation yet. What they learn from their coaches, they will carry forward to the generations to come.

At every stage of development, the coach is an example to the players, and a coach's role is critical, no less so in the tech age of today.

By the way, I adore Tiger and believe I could help him win more majors!

Chapter 5
Snowflakes

Winning Strategy:

Understand you are extraordinary!

What does it take to be great? First, dismiss the idea of being merely great. Think extraordinary! We all have extraordinary moments in our extraordinary lives. There is no such thing as mediocrity. In order to self-actualize fully, it takes fuel, fortitude and momentum for growth, and the more momentum the better.

Without vision, the people perish. Added to vision, persistence carries the torch when one faces stubborn obstacles and setbacks. Steadfast perseverance is a powerful force when reaching the goal is a long-time in the making. Another element key to building momentum on the path to being extraordinary is taking a kind stance with the naysayers. Go ahead and major in "un-limitations," and keep going, no matter what others think or say.

I discovered the secret to extraordinary existence years before becoming a coach. This was in fourth grade, which was ecstasy! After spending a little less than two weeks in third grade, terrorizing the teacher, the school promoted me to fourth grade featuring Mr. Wood, a most remarkable man indeed. If asked what he looked like, my memory pictures him as a twin of Bryan Cranston, the actor playing Mr. White, a science teacher-turned-drug-dealer in the award winning "Breaking Bad" series.

The man had character. His mind was electric and inventive, and he could not care less about social recognition, especially when it came to me, an angry but wildly imaginative troublemaker. Mr. Wood's specialties were science and math. Among the many other fascinating things he did, he ended class a few minutes early to challenge us with verbal math problems. Two plus nine, minus three, times five, plus seven? POW! (Answer: 47!) In a nanosecond my hand shot up with the answer, flawless every time.

One day we put aside the books and he held up an ice ball, something all my friends and I knew a lot about. Alongside the ice ball he held up a large photograph of a snowflake. Then he asked the question, "How many snowflakes do you think there are in this ice ball?"

Guesses reigned supreme until he revealed that there were a little less than one million snowflakes in a baseball-sized ice ball. POW! Amazement flashed in and out of my mind.

First, how in the world could a snowflake be photographed? Secondly, how did he get them into the ice ball? Then he blew us all out of the room when he claimed that "NO TWO SNOWFLAKES WERE ALIKE!" Double POW! The fourth grade was one of the first turning points of my life. Mr. Wood was my first real hero, and he was my hero then and he is still my hero today!

Here's the thing. Extraordinary people, like Mr. Wood, live with an authentic spirit and inspire others. They don't have to be perfect, or glamorous, or anything but themselves. They just need to know how to connect with people and see the value and potential in encouraging others to realize that they, too, are extraordinary.

Chapter 6
Dynamite

Winning strategy:

Victories are first won in the mind.

At Northwest Soccer Camp, the kids call me Uncle Nubby and my former players and even closest friends call me Nubber. I like the sound of that. At this point, those who have not met me in person may be wondering, "Who is this Uncle Nubby character?"

It's a story that goes back to 1944 and an event that changed the course of my life, or at least some of the things I would learn about life. Here's what happened. When I was eight years old, I blew off two fingers and a thumb from my left hand with a dynamite cap. It was October and we were in Canada, where my mother's family lived. It all started with a game of hide and seek.

Brother Paul is "It" and Cliffy, (that's me) darted into an implement shed to hide. Knowing intuitively I would be trapped trying to hide behind an implement (a tool or piece of equipment), a quick survey revealed a stepladder made of two-by-fours allowing access to another two-by-four stretching overhead from side to side of the shed.

I climbed the makeshift ladder and there, on the ledge was a greasy, lidless box cradling what looked like a dozen or so spent gun shells. I perched midway waiting for brother Paul Bernard McCrath to appear. It wasn't long before the silent vigil ended with the arrival of the "It!" I had the escape plan well rehearsed in my mind: When Paul Bernard looked up, I would plummet to the ground from my perch and easily run home free.

I watched him search behind plows, barrels and even under dust canopies covering who-knows-what. Paul then drifted back to the open space just below my perch above. From where I was hiding, I could have reached down and flicked off his cap. Then he was gone, having never looked up.

The Box! I managed to rotate my body and ease my way back to the ledge to snatch one of the "shells" previously eyed in The Box. I held it in my mouth during a smooth descent then put it in the right pocket of my pants where it would remain for two days.

The next night, some 10 miles south, there was a family birthday party with a cake. Tradition called for the candles to be lit by the youngest, who was me. I was also whining and insisting on getting to light the candles because I was wanting to grab a few extra matches.

The next day was a crisp October day, perfect for outdoor play. While the adults were reveling as most reunions inspired, my brother and I were doing our usual snooping around when Paul Bernard announced he had an emergency message from "below."

He then made a beeline for the rickety outhouse. Once PB was ensconced, I promptly turned the external, wooden knob and locked him inside to ensure he would be incarcerated long enough to SAS (snitch a smoke). I ambled over to the corner of the garage adjacent to the house out of viewing range of any house dweller.

It is at this point a brief retreat a little further into the past is required. During the war years, there was no age requirement for kids to go into taverns with their folks - or even just wandering in to steal sips of beer, cigarette butts or play a little shuffleboard until kicked out. Inasmuch as there was no Disneyland at that time, it was in such a place where I got my first visit to "Wonderland."

A typical scene was a table surrounded by four men - all smoking, sipping beer or other liquids - while playing euchre - the game of choice in those days. The kids, between shuffles, would spot near-empty beer bottles and approach a given table pining for an opportunity to drain the last inch or two of stale beer.

Sometimes one of the men would drop a match or cigarette butt into an empty bottle. This caused the kids to stand mesmerized watching the captured smoke do a slow "Flight of the Bumblebee" dance trying to escape the bottle. Clearly, such mystery had etched its way into to the deepest regions of my brain.

With my older brother Paul locked in the outhouse, it was when reaching for the matches that my hand felt what I thought was the shell. The urge to light up was replaced with a desire to recreate the smoke-in-the-bottle trick. Holding the "shell" (actually a dynamite cap) in my left thumb and first two fingers, I lit the match and attempted to insert it.

Over the next several minutes, Hell paid a brief visit to Southern Ontario!

Forget smoke in a bottle! A bomb caused the earth to move and, if anybody had been watching, the outhouse probably moved 10 feet from its mooring as well.

The blast was so loud, people came running out of the house as if needing to run for the hills. I was standing with my eyes to the sky convinced a bowling ball had rolled off the roof and hit me in the head. (See bomb effects!) In any event, the people, with horrified looks, began vigorously patting my sweater that was on fire. In addition, my face, minus eyebrows and eyelashes, was a sea of blood gushing from multiple open wounds from the shrapnel that peppered my face, neck and everything else above my armpits!

It was at that moment I began pointing at the outhouse from which furious pounding sounds were coming. Comically, if there was any humor in what was happening, the people began tiptoeing toward the outhouse. Perhaps they assumed the inhabitant was the perpetrator of whatever had just happened. With great apprehension, they loosened the outer bolt, allowing the frightful looking older brother to escape. Within seconds, he was face-to-face with me and, for the first time in my memory, I witnessed Paul Bernard crying. He was the first to observe that my left hand was missing something.

According to Homer McLay, the doctor who tidied up the mess with a very special three-hour amputation, I came dangerously close to losing my eyesight, if not my life. The whole episode provides some insight into why the mind matters.

It was now time for the mind to enter stage left and begin its work to make the best of overcoming the challenge often labeled "handicap," "disabled," or worse. To relearn how to tie shoes and button shirts was an obstacle most eight year olds never have to consider. As for how the mind engaged and managed this, as with many of life's challenges, it needed an ally. In my case, it was a rock of a woman, my mother Dorcas, who came to the rescue.

Early on, when I came home in tears from a neighborhood baseball game, excluded because I was "a freak of nature," she was ready. She sat me down and opened a folder containing several clippings from newspapers and magazines. She read stories of people who lost their hands in the war and learned to play the violin by taping a bow to a stub of an arm or learned to type with their toes. (Helen Keller got Center Stage billing.)

Dorcas followed such awesome stories with a few of her own, ending with, "You can now make a choice: Go through life sitting in a corner with a sock over your hand or learn to use your nubs and other two fingers the same way or better than those with 10 fingers." SHAZAAM!

The business of "choosing one's attitude" is the sole province of the mind. As a coach, this is a valuable lesson to impart because it makes all the difference in the world between an individual's success or failure. What I learned from this experience is that there are going to be losses in life, some harder to accept than others, but more importantly, victories are first won in the mind.

Chapter 7
Tell Me About That

Winning Strategy:
Make course corrections when needed.

In addition to being a soccer coach, I'm also an ordained minister and counselor to students and couples, so I've seen people struggle with the same problems time and again. It's as common today as it was 50 years ago for people to be stubborn in doing things their way, even when it is clearly not working at all. Perhaps there is at least one area of every person's life like this.

What I say to people who come to talk about these issues is this. "Well, you must like the results you are getting if you keep doing things the same way. Why don't you tell me about that?"

The ability to learn from mistakes will help every person, coach, couple, and business manager. In fact, it could help our country, too. From what I see,

40

the world is reeling. What I'd most like to tell the world is to change directions. It's not this way – it's that way.

However, never criticize a player without giving a solution!

One way to turn things around, according to the famous Coach John Wooden of UCLA fame, is to make practice much more difficult than any game. The subtext is that by working harder, things get easier and excellence becomes natural and easy. It's not just that practice makes perfect, it's that practice makes permanent, (and I will discuss that again, later).

Some people, and strong athletes, have enough creativity that they only need to be given the principles, and they can take it from there. My grandson Keith, for example (my daughter Stacey's son), plays college basketball and his father was a professional basketball player. He may be too, someday.

I took him to lunch before college and while we were sitting there, I said, "As a basketball player, you may think I don't know anything about basketball." Then I proceeded to tell him two things. First, "I'm available," and second, "No tattoos." What are grandfathers for?

I noticed that when he shoots, his basketball says, "I hope," not, "Ball's going in." I pointed that out. When I support someone on becoming a person, I'm specific, not just "good job, good job," as is more common nowadays.

His nickname when he was younger was KC, for Keith Charles (before he was Little Keith, because Keith is also his father's name), but since then I gave him the new nickname of "Angry."

"Angry, when you shoot, follow through with your hand down and then turn and run back, knowing it went in. Take 10,000 shots, practice."

He probably doesn't know this, but I was an angry kid myself. Although in the early years, I was given to fits of rage, eventually I absorbed my mother's mastery of emotions.

Christians often say, "Jesus is the answer," but since the night I chased a cheerleader into an evangelistic tent meeting, and converted to Christianity, Jesus has been my problem. But to be fair, the role He has played in my life changed the rage that once controlled my actions into a surprising calm.

I'm not sure how it all works, but there came a time when I was able to access immediately my innermost feelings. Instead of irrational behavior, I seemed always to press the pause button and surface from potentially damaging situations in control. Those who know me well, (such as my friend Denise), say, "He is at his best when we are at our worst."

Scripture says, "A soft (quiet) word turns away wrath, but a harsh word stirs up anger!"

I'm also passionate about history and quotations. One of my favorites that I credit for some of the calm demeanor came from the 18th Century: "A fine preaching has he been at the night…but maybe least said is soonest mended." ~ "Heart of Midlothian," by Sir Walter Scott.

There came a time when I took an internal inventory and it occurred to me that trying to explain every nuance of my behavior took too much energy. In addition, there were situations where my impulsive actions together with my anger and hot-headedness always resulted in loss of freedom and emotional torment leading to one dead-end after another.

One such graphic experience was at Camp Brookwoods in New Hampshire where I worked for many summers during and after college. A fellow counselor challenged me to a game of tennis. Although I knew just a little about tennis, I felt he was a bit of a wimp, so within seconds I agreed to the challenge. The problem was, I didn't own a racket, so I borrowed a nice one from one of the campers. We played, and the other staff member proceeded to win. Because of this, I flew into a rage whacking the racket against one of the posts holding up the fence to the court.

What I didn't know about the intricacies of the game was miniscule compared to what I didn't know about a stringed (taut) tennis racket. The catgut bands of the racket popped like a pail full of firecrackers on the 4th of

July. The shock that no amount of ingenuity could repair the mess in my hand brought my way of managing life's challenges to a screeching halt.

After apologizing to the kid and paying (plenty) for his racket, it occurred to me that something had to change. My only regret is that I didn't keep the broken racket to hang in my trophy case as one of the better artifacts of achievement.

Chapter 8
A Coach's Rewards

Winning Strategy:

Look to rewards for the greater good.

The Taj Mahal is a World Heritage Site in India inspired by a great love story and an emperor who felt compelled to act. The stimulus of it was a moral imperative, which is the Divine voice speaking through the human spirit.

If a coach expects personal glory and is motivated solely by "What's In It For Me," as a matter of course, I don't want to have anything to do with this manner of coaching. In business, WIIFM is death to team performance. No matter what the venue for leadership (e.g. office, home, school or athletic field), one's purpose must be greater than personal glory.

A coach's rewards are three-fold: 1) The result of the effort; 2) A better night's sleep; 3) Relationships with people that last a lifetime.

Players will play harder for the coach who has a higher purpose in mind. In the corporate world, employees are motivated in this way, too. These days, when I'm invited to present keynote speeches on coaching, I share that the definition of success is the moral validation of a challenge. When one chooses to do something based on the moral imperative, this type of judgment is influenced by intuition (the inner voice, or Spirit) combined with controlled reasoning. Economic moral imperatives, for example, lead to decisions about how to help the most people with finite resources.

Anson Dorrance is the coach of the University of North Carolina's women's soccer team. Under his guidance, the team has won 21 of 31 NCAA Women's Soccer Championships. He is one of the NCAA's most winning coaches and he was coach of the U.S. Women's first world championship team in 1991. He is the person I have been quoted as calling "simply the best soccer coach on the planet."

I interviewed him on video before presenting him as the Coach's Choice for the Honor Award (the highest award in soccer). I asked him the secret of his success and he said, "It's my moral imperative to be the very best at what I do!"

On another occasion, Os Guinness, an Oxford-educated scholar, came to speak on campus at Seattle Pacific. It was a great opportunity to hear from one of the brightest minds in the world. (Guinness, born to missionary parents in China, is the great-great-great grandson of Arthur Guinness, the Dublin brewer.) His definition of culture was that it is magnanimous, mysterious and subtle. Culture is man's creative activity within God-given structure. Guinness went on to draft the Global Charter of Conscience for the European Union in 2014, which is a global covenant concerning faith and freedom of conscience.

Freedom of conscience is the right to follow one's own beliefs in matters of religion and morality. This manifests in many ways. For example, when we stand (or don't stand) for the national anthem before a sporting event in America, we are honoring (or dishonoring) people who served the country. The soldiers who paid a huge sacrifice for all of us did not ask, "What's in it for me?" By standing, we are honoring those heroes.

Certainly, when the United States is not living up to its ideals, it is our First Amendment right to protest. But refusing to stand for the anthem, by being disrespectful to people who served the country, who are of all races and religions, gets in the way of the message. If the moral imperative compels one to act, best judgment requires finding the most constructive way to do it in seeking rewards for the greater good.

Chapter 9
Northwest Soccer Camp

Winning Strategy:

Let kids learn from their peers.

Northwest Soccer Camp became part of my life work in 1972 and continues to this day, 47 years later. In the early years, I took my own children, Stacey and Steve, with me to camp, as they were just the right age to join in the fun. Over time, many of the young campers became camp counselors and then camp coaches, later some played professionally, or went on to coach college soccer.

In 1972, there were 6,000 youths playing recreational soccer in Washington, like what represents the foundation of sports throughout the world. There were no professional teams in the Northwest yet and thus the college teams were highly visible to the young players. The Seattle Pacific Falcons had just made the national playoffs for the first time, and local people took notice because no school in the area had ever done that. It didn't take much insight to figure out why my phone was ringing off the hook, and parents began visiting my office to get soccer tutoring.

Many parent-coaches were just learning about the game at the same time as their kids and that was really exciting. I loved to see the momentum and skill level grow year-by-year. By the next summer, Northwest Soccer Camp added parent coaching camp, and this helped accelerate the growth of soccer in the Pacific Northwest. It wasn't too long before the number of youth soccer players in Washington grew to 100,000, beginning the Northwest domination of the sport.

I should mention, some of the parent-coaches in the rec leagues didn't need any tutoring at all. They were from soccer-playing countries, which meant that in the early stages of soccer in the Northwest, their kids had a leg up on other kids new to the sport (pun intended).

In Seattle, many of the top coaches in the early days were from Europe. Some were engineers at Boeing, foundry workers, or practiced other skilled trades. My Irish friend Mike Ryan, the UW coach, came to Seattle in 1962, where he discovered a vibrant scene of European teams and a carnival atmosphere of singing and picnics around Sunday games with spectators six deep. Hungarians, Germans, Russians and other ethnic teams played and Ed

Craggs (who I met with Ryan on my first day in Seattle), published the soccer news with lineups and scores.

Midge and I came to the Northwest not knowing what to expect from the local soccer scene, but already accustomed to the excellence of Europeans players. When I coached in Boston, the Gordon team's high scorer was a Greek "god" named Pantelis "Paul" Sideropoulos, at one time the career-leading scorer (108 goals) in collegiate history. Americans were late to adopt the game, and we had a lot of catching up to do.

At Northwest Soccer Camp, we learned a great deal about coaching young players, both boys and girls, from beginner to elite level. The style of coaching was never autocratic. Instead, we let the kids learn from each other, spend time on the ball, and get encouragement from drills with the coaches. This is more akin to modern-day coaching styles than to the negative reinforcement that was customary then (screaming, insulting and belittling players was all-too common).

Spanning five decades of directing the camp, much of what I learned is about how to coach different age groups, which varies considerably from one age to the next. For example, children 12-years-old and up demand explanation and expert demonstration followed by participation, correction and honest feedback. In no way can the coach wing it by this stage of development.

Even for younger children who are just learning basic skills, teaching how to pass a ball correctly is a carefully orchestrated process reinforced by repetition and discovery and further practice. The young players need to feel "aha...I can do it!" A seven-year old's attention span is seven seconds. Therefore, I learned that we teach best by play. Perhaps I was even a bit of a pioneer in this approach.

Rather than announcing to a group of children, "We're going to learn passing," there is another way of learning that is innate and works better. During a drill that involves a difficult new skill, most of the kids will get discouraged, but a few will succeed. At this point, we say, "Try it the way little Johnny or Susie is doing it," and this works because kids learn more from their peers than from their coaches!

In teaching little kids, I also like to use the Oreo cookie idea, starting with positive feedback before bringing in the critique. A lot of parents and teachers bring in the criticism, and that causes them to lose the child's attention. Think plus, minus, plus: positive comment, then constructive criticism, then add a plus at the end by giving more positive response about what is being done right. It works like a charm, but above all, let kids learn from their peers as much as possible.

Chapter 10
Scout

Winning Strategy:

Do What's Best, Not What's Easiest.

Once my Falcons made it to the national championships, Seattle was abuzz. This and Northwest Soccer Camp helped raise awareness of soccer in the Seattle area in the early 1970s, but there was much more going on behind the scenes.

Enter Walt Daggatt, a well-known businessman and public figure in Seattle.

Walt was the "gunner" for the Skinner Corp, co-founder of the original Seattle Professional Sports (SPS) holding group. The Skinner Corporation, led by industrialist David "Ned" Skinner II, (1920-1988), apparently owned half of Seattle, including Alpac Bottling (later Pepsi Bottling) among its vast empire.

Skinner cofounded SPS with entrepreneur Herman Sarkowsky, owner of the Portland Trailblazers and Seattle's top real estate developer. They brought in majority stakeholder Lloyd Nordstrom, the department store mogul of the Nordstrom Group, (a family of enormous wealth and prestige in Seattle). Other Who's Who members included retail magnate M. Lamar "Monte" Bean, developer Howard S. Wright, and Hotelier Lynn Himmelman.

Daggatt set out on behalf of SPS to get the blessing of the National Football League headquartered in Dallas for an expansion team. Although the initial goal was a professional football franchise, in the end soccer came to Seattle first. This was likely an understood prerequisite for the consortium, according to the following story.

On the way to Dallas to bring an NFL franchise home, Daggatt met a man in Scottsdale, Arizona. This man, resembling a middle-aged accountant, was none other than oil heir Lamar Hunt, owner of the Dallas Tornado, a North American Soccer League (NASL) pro team. He was also the founder of the American Football League (AFL) that merged with the National Football League (NFL) in 1970. Thus, in addition to his NASL team, Hunt was the owner of the Kansas City Chiefs football team (which he founded as the Dallas Texans in 1960).

Hunt became a strong advocate for soccer in the U.S. after seeing the FIFA World Cup games in England in 1966. When he returned to the states, he immediately founded the Dallas Tornado (1967), one of nine soccer teams in the NASL. The team's roster included mostly European players, who set off on a world tour in 1967-68, playing games in 26 countries on five continents for crowds as large as 50,000.

When Walt Daggatt and Lamar Hunt met, the conversation between the two men went along the lines of Hunt saying, "While you are waiting for a football franchise, try soccer."

Walt interpreted these words as a mandate to do soccer first, and he brought this information back to SPS. Following the meeting with Hunt, the group commissioned Daggatt to gather facts about the possible success of pro soccer on the path to approval for an NFL team. Soon after, he called a meeting inviting eight soccer coaches to lunch at Horatio's, a restaurant in the AGC Building, along with sports executive Dick Vertlieb and representatives of the holding company.

Herman Sarkowsky, owner of the Portland Trailblazers, occupied the ninth floor of the building where we met. Incidentally, this was 1972, and the building itself was a state-of-the-art concrete skyscraper on Lake Union, completed in 1971. (Today, 22 high-rise Amazon buildings surround it.) It is the Seattle headquarters of Associated General Contractors.

The two German coaches at the table were Boeing engineers who came to Seattle to assist the company in postwar expansion. They stayed and, of course, in their leisure time, pursued their native sport (art form?) by playing and introducing soccer to locals as well as providing an outlet for their own kids. Hence, the early formalization of the Washington State Youth Soccer Association in the 1960s.

Fellow Boeing colleagues Tom Webb, Robin Chalmers and Jack Goldingay joined the two Germans (Karl Grosch and Karl Heinz-Schreiber) at the table. Mike Ryan, an Irishman, coached the University of Washington's men's soccer team and I was the coach for Seattle Pacific.

This meeting is vivid in my mind to this day, although many of the key founding businessmen and coaches have passed away. Goldingay, who started early youth soccer teams in Washington, died in 1993 at age 80. Dick Vertlieb died in 2008, Walt Daggatt died age 91 in 2010, Mike Ryan died in 2012, and Herman Sarkowsky died in 2014, age 89.

Walt Daggatt was a gentleman who rarely raised his voice. He was a chain smoker and wouldn't flick his ash. Dick Vertlieb had a handlebar moustache and smoked a pipe. He was the general manager of the Seattle Super Sonics, and later for the Golden State Warriors (in 1975 he was named NBA Executive of the Year). He also helped found the Portland Trailblazers with Herman Sarkowsky.

Sarkowsky fled Germany as a child with his Jewish family in 1934, first to New York and then to Seattle in 1937. By 1950, he was in the homebuilding business. By the 1960s, he was the most successful real estate developer in Seattle's history.

Eventually Dick said, "We should hire Cliff to put the soccer team together, because we don't know a damn thing about soccer."

The working idea at that stage was to bring traveling teams to Seattle and get 6,000 people to attend the games at Memorial Stadium. After the meeting, Walt Daggatt, the organizer, asked me to stay behind.

"There were eight guys down there, why me?" I asked.

"Because you're the only one who speaks English!" he said. (I presume he meant American English.)

This was a tough decision in my life, and my first professional coaching offer. There was a serious consequence to consider because the National

Collegiate Athletic Association (NCAA), which governs college sports, didn't permit coaches to take a stipend or any form of professional athletic pay. Nowadays, stipends fall in the gray area, but there was no gray area in the 1970s. I thought of my family's security. If I took the pro post, it would mean giving up my job at Seattle Pacific.

Thinking of my family, I chose to go with the more stable of the two, and that meant staying in college soccer. Yes, the glory of a professional team would have been great! However, with a young family at the time, my position at Seattle Pacific was more important. Midge and I had worked hard for more than a decade for the stability, home and professional careers we had achieved. I could not risk our family's well-being.

I stood up, ready to say goodbye, but Walt didn't give up. Instead, he sent me to Philadelphia and then to Dallas to sit down with Lamar Hunt, which I did. Hunt and I went over the books of his soccer team and discussed elements of the 1966 World Cup Games in England (that England won), which we both happened to attend, though several years before our meeting. Ticket sales were very important in England at that time.

Following our meeting, I wrote a detailed seven-page pro forma report for Seattle, forecasting $1.41 per ticket including a city tax with an average of

6,000 fans. I gave the report to Walt Daggatt upon my return, but he pushed it aside.

"We want you to do the whole thing," he said. As incentive, they offered a six-figure salary, car, and benefits.

"I don't think this league will last," was my blunt, but honest reply, made with much thought and weighed consideration packed into the statement.

We settled on me doing the color commentary for the TV games, providing the expert analysis and humor that "add color" to the commentary of the play-by-play announcer. I then set out to recruit the players for the Seattle Sounders, the name of the new team. They came mostly from England, and specifically the English Premier League, then known as Division 1. I also found a couple of Dutch players, all the best of the best. Initially, we housed the players at Seattle Pacific.

I recruited the Sounders' first general manger, Jack Daley, a huge man serving as publicist for the Toronto Metros, one of four teams to make it to the playoffs in 1973. I met him while scouting the Atom's semifinal game in Philadelphia. He heard I was the "Seattle guy" and followed me around for three days. When I turned down the job of running the Sounders, I recommended him as GM and John Best (the Dallas captain) as coach.

By 1974, the Seattle Sounders kicked off its first season. Attendance soared, the first home game sold out, and by mid-year, we shipped in 5,000 more seats. Soon the holding group, with Herman Sarkowsky as CEO, succeeded in bringing a pro football team to Seattle.

The NFL awarded the football franchise to Seattle Professional Football (majority stakeholder Nordstrom and minority stakeholders Sarkowsky, Skinner, Bean, Howard, and Himmelman) on December 5, 1974.

I used to cite all the names but more recently simply refer to the group as The Nordstrom Group. I was with them all at the Washington Athletic Club the morning they were reviewing the first season of the Sounders. Lloyd Nordstrom came late to breakfast, never sat down, stated he was leaving for vacation in Mexico, but before he left said, "I just have this to say, the Sounders is simply the best investment I ever made and I recommend we sell!"

The next news we received, he died of a heart attack playing tennis in Mexico! He didn't live long enough to see the first NFL pro football exhibition game played in the Kingdome, which was the Seattle Seahawks versus the San Francisco 49ers on August 1, 1976.

The NASL Sounders folded at the end of the 1983 season and the league itself died in 1984. The Sounders team name was later revived, more than a quarter of a century later, for the new pro soccer team in Seattle. In 2010, I received the Golden Scarf Award from the new Seattle Sounders FC. This was for my work as a scout for the original team and for continued involvement in the growth of soccer in Seattle and the Northwest for 40 years.

Chapter 11
Coaching the Real Kid

Winning Strategy:

Make a lifelong impact.

Each summer, I bid farewell to city life and Midge, and headed to Whidbey Island with the kids for Northwest Soccer Camp, followed by Seattle Pacific's pre-season training in August. The island lies in the rain shadow of the Olympic Mountain Range and is one of the most beautiful places in the world.

It was common for as many as 75 college students to turn out for 24 positions on the team, meaning I would have to cut more than 50 kids at the end of the tryouts. Of those players who made the team, some could have been stars for other schools, but ended up on the bench for the Falcons, which had become a national championship-level team.

The competition to be on the team was fierce and grueling for the college athletes, so the curfew, normally, was never an issue. Most were more than ready to fall asleep after two-a-day practices in the summer heat. Not only were they exhausted, but also to get on and off the island required taking a ferry, which was a bit of an ordeal.

One year, however, four of the guys broke the curfew rule, and consequently ended up with black marks against their names before final cuts for the team were made. One of the curfew-breakers, a talented player, was (in my opinion) a pisser kid full of moxy and a contrarian to me and other coaches. Perhaps because he was challenging the coach's wisdom (in setting a curfew), I decided to cut him, although this was more of a knee-jerk reaction than a rational decision.

Looking back, if I had it to do again, I would not do the same thing; hindsight is 20/20. I realize now that if I had been consistent, this young man wouldn't have disappeared into the woodwork. He may have become a professional player. He would not have carried disappointment and bitterness with him through life, as I imagine may have happened.

I learned from that lesson, and in order to avoid that kind of mistake ever again, I never put a kid on the bench or cut him from the team again for not liking him. I also made it a rule not to tell a player he wasn't good enough, although perhaps I would say he was not yet strong enough to play at that level.

As a soccer player myself, there was one game when Coach B. taught me the lesson of respect. For three years at Wheaton, I played every minute of every game except one minute when he held me out for yelling at the referee. Since I have been the kid with an attitude, it gives me some insight into what works and what does not.

Another "real kid" attitude issue I've dealt with as a coach is "grades-in-the-toilet" players. Sometimes, the best players don't even bother to go to class. For younger kids, they may end up going to the principal's office every day, like I did. In some cases, the sport the real kid loves can be what saves his academic career.

A word of caution, though. One of the worst things a kid can hear is, "You've got so much potential." To that, they will say, "I'm going to try to work harder," but all that does is foster lip service and no achievements.

As an alternative, I say to them, "You must be very happy with the decisions you are making because you do it over and over again."

They may then say, "Well maybe I'm not as good at that as I think I am."

At that point, they will help provide answers about what they are going to do differently, buying into the idea that they must replace behaviors creating a messy and unsuccessful life. It's a different kind of order. (I discuss this further in the chapter "Practice Makes Permanent.")

This way of talking and thinking applies to all areas of life and makes an enduring impact. It calls attention to the fact that "trying" is not actually "doing" things differently. Trying creates the possibility of failure, whereas doing is an ongoing action of success.

"Do or Do not. There is no try."

~ Jedi Master Yoda, *The Empire Strikes Back* (story by George Lucas).

Chapter 12
Key Ingredients

Winning Strategy:

Know what you know.

Great achievers never accept society's definition of what can and can't be done. They don't allow artificial barriers or abide by someone else defining who they are. Achievers ignore the naysayers, who are those people who want others to believe they are not special or that something can't be done.

Great achievers base what they do on who they are, not the other way around. Too often, we default into accepting that what a person does is more important than who a person is. Yet growth from within is going to continue throughout life, regardless of occupation, political interests, or other one-dimensional descriptions. The inner self knows how to continue to grow, unfold and be alive.

I memorized "tons" of scripture in the years 1954 to 1960, as well as massive amounts of arcane information that some might view as "dead facts." I also believe I can discern, intuitively, when people are faking it, lying, putting on a show for others, sad, in pain, and needy. I know by heart the whisperings of my own heart, and when emotions are driving actions, and, I can access the nature of emotion within seconds. I have learned how to defuse and reconcile issues.

During an argument, I instantly recognize whether I am to blame and can remedy it (in contrast to my early years) lifting the burden from the other person. In short, I don't stay angry or need to "win" the argument. This skill has helped me resolve conflicts with others who seem to benefit from me saying, "Do you want to win the argument or find a solution?"

What else do I know? On a lighter note, let me tell you about a few of the favorite dishes I like to cook. One is my salmon on a variety of beds served more on the medium rare to rare side (succulent). The beds include the usual rice, except mine is always brown rice from Trader Joe's frozen section, and it cooks in the microwave in three minutes and 47 seconds. The last few seconds added time is to puff the bag and ensure proper cooking. Another option is a bed of Brussel sprouts and the final surprise is Robert Rothschild's Roasted Pineapple and Habanero Glaze and Finishing Sauce – alone, without any underpinning. The awesome, amazing revelation is that I do it all in the microwave!

Another dish is my chicken curry, which is comprised of just six ingredients. One, of course, is chicken breasts sliced into small bites, the other ingredients include Madras Curry Powder, red pepper flakes, garlic, coconut milk or light cream and chutney.

I also make a Nub Salad that people crow about. I never make two the same way, but people love it. The salad has quite a few cheeses, tomatoes, avocados (sliced and cubed), usually romaine lettuce, but lately I toss in some kale and arugula...a touch of avocado oil, balsamic, topped with parmesan flakes or grated parmesan to die for!

This delicious salad makes a great metaphor for finding one's personal coaching style and other secrets for success through personal growth. The ingredients in a person that come together to make a great coach may not necessarily have anything to do with a strict coaching recipe *per se.* Allow room for experimentation and learn from mistakes and strokes of genius for best results.

Chapter 13

Fears and Regrets

Winning strategy:

Learn to laugh at yourself.

Here's a question I was asked recently: "What fears or regrets must people learn to put aside to succeed?"

Quick answer: All of them!

Am I perfect? Am I a choirboy on Heaven's Honor Roll? No. But there is no room in my mind for fear and regret if I want to achieve and enjoy living the life of my dreams. God's view of us is that we are accepted. I choose to accept myself, and sometimes to laugh at myself when things get cockeyed.

In general, I'm not given to regrets about paths not taken, or decisions gone awry. Fears and regrets are cancerous bedfellows that wreak havoc on the human spirit by eating away all that is positive, creative and needed for victorious living.

I have learned two sound principles: (1) Get back on the horse after a fall, and (2) Learn to laugh at trouble.

The first principle is what I share with my teams after a painful defeat:

"You're allowed to grieve for three seconds, then we begin preparing for the next game."

The second principle is something that's both funny and true:

"If you're going to play with dynamite, do not play with matches at the same time!" Obviously, that's how I lost two fingers and a thumb, which I don't want to see anyone else do.

One of the examples I love of fearlessness combined with a sense of humor is John McKay, the incredibly successful former head football coach at University of Southern California from 1960 to 1975. His team, the USC Trojans, had two losing seasons when he first arrived, and he came close to getting fired. USC gave him another year, and his teams thereafter won four national championships in 1962, 1967, 1972 and 1974. He was voted National Coach of the Year twice in 1962 and 1972.

After this enormously successful career, he left college football to go pro, moving across the country to coach the Tampa Bay Buccaneers. He left USC, he said, because he "wanted to make some money -- it's that simple.'" As college coach and athletic director, he was earning $48,000 a year. His first pro contract gave him $750,000 over five years, $250,000 in Florida real estate and life-insurance policies for him and his wife. The money was very respectable.

However, the Buccaneers were a fledgling team, and in those days, few good players were available in the NFL expansion draft. Free agency did not yet exist, so McKay started with little talent. His team proceeded to lose 26 games in a row and his reputation as a winning coach was in grave jeopardy. After one of those losses, when he was asked what he thought of his team's execution, he replied, "I think it's a good idea." When asked when his team would win a game, he said, "Only God knows, and I'm not too close to God now."

He coached the Tampa Bay Buccaneers from 1976 through 1984. After the Buccaneers defeated the New Orleans Saints for their first win in 1977, McKay joked, "Three or four plane crashes and we're in the playoffs." It wasn't until his fourth season, in 1979, that the Bucs won their division title.

They won it again in 1981, and in all, three of his teams qualified for the playoffs.

It's essential to hold on to a sense of humor and what is more, it's the hallmark of a champion.

Chapter 14
Muscle Memory

Winning Strategy:

Practice Makes Permanent.

Do concentration and focus in practice make a big difference come game day? Of course. Does a ballet dancer need to practice her/his twirls or just run out on stage and begin hopping and pirouetting? Does driver's education class help a 16-year-old new driver avoid the ditches? Practice does not make perfect, it makes permanent!

If what is being practiced is the correct repetition, practice is paramount to peak performance. For many tactile exercises, such as most sports, practice is the gateway to muscle-memory, which sets apart precision performances from failure. Muscle memory is the ability to perform a movement without conscious thought, and this is based on frequent repetition of the movement. It may sound like a new idea, but the more old-fashioned term for it was motor learning.

Muscle memory (or motor learning) decreases the need for attention and takes over in the heat-of-battle to execute desired results that represent the difference between victory or defeat.

There are internal "muscles" as well, including emotions, mental acuity, and spiritual reserves. I learned to exercise these internal muscles in seminary from Dr. Lloyd Perry, Professor of Homiletics at Gordon Divinity School (now Gordon-Conwell Theological Seminary). He believed a successful preacher should spend one hour in preparation for every minute of sermon. The practice part of his formula tallied 20 hours for a 20-minute sermon.

According to Dr. Perry, the preacher must write out the sermon, then convert it to 3" x 5" cards, then throw the cards away and get up and preach. His point being that a clear and memorable sermon should be well-prepared and have strong points, easily remembered by those hearing it for the first time. If a preacher does not remember his own sermon after 20 hours of preparation (using the cards as a crutch), the congregation should not be expected to remember it either.

Earlier, when I was at Wheaton, I attended Wheaton Bible Church where Malcom Cronk was pastor. (In appearance, he was a twin of the Penguin in Batman, but one of the greatest preachers I ever heard.) His formula for preaching was, "Read yourself full, pray yourself hot, preach yourself empty!"

Growing up, several adages became part of my arsenal used in life's challenges. Later, I discarded some due to their folly or reworked them to become critical weapons to combat formidable enemies. These foes included mediocrity, slothfulness and outright withdrawal (quitting, giving up or bailing out). One, of the adages that I had to rework was "practice makes perfect!"

I'm not sure exactly when it occurred to me, but my lifelong insistence on truth and justice always led me to challenge people, situations, and concepts. "Practice makes perfect" was one of the more threadbare utterances that fell quickly when my inner analytics concluded that all the practice in the world would/could not make me perfect.

Indeed, the harder I tried to achieve personal perfection and the more pressure I exerted on my players and workers to do the same, the clearer it became that the results were rarely perfect. At that point, I began to dig deeper, reading voraciously and observing people in the public and private sectors who seemed to be flawless in their performances. I began asking questions of successful people. The scripture says, "In a multitude of counselors there is wisdom."

After this exploration, I changed the adage "practice makes perfect" to suit my newfound insights. Hence, "Practice doesn't make perfect; it makes permanent!"

As part of the student personnel office and coach of the men's soccer team at Gordon, it wasn't long before my new philosophy reached those entrusted to my care. One example that jumps out at me came up frequently with players and students in trouble academically. Invariably, they would appear before me to provide rationale(s) as to why they should be allowed to continue as students or soccer players.

One year, a junior who had already missed a year of playing time due to academic ineligibility, promised he would work harder and do better next term.

"Bullsh*t!" I said, no doubt shocking him. "You have repeated the same behavior and patterns for several terms, which means trying harder obviously doesn't work. What you really need to do is change your thinking!"

We forged a new routine for him (a new "practice") that led to an amazing turnaround and a spectacular career (still going) in the medical field.

One last disclaimer: Practice may make perfect, but what is being practiced MUST be the right stuff!

Chapter 15
Tough Choices

Winning Strategy:

Compassion.

While playing golf recently with a couple of former players and assistant coaches of yesteryear, one said, "I still use the principle you taught us in camp."

Knowing there are about 47 principles I may have shared at any one time, I asked, "Which one?"

He said, "The principle about using compassion when cutting a player."

The other fellow looked at us and said, "I use that principle, too.

What they were talking about is something I call "The two o'clock game and the five o'clock ferry." That's shorthand for something that happened at Camp Casey during preseason training one year.

Camp Casey is a picturesque place to spend time outdoors, located next to Fort Casey State Park on Whidbey Island in the northern part of Puget Sound. As I mentioned earlier, I spent many summers on the island because in addition to preseason training, this is where we held Northwest Soccer Camp for 38 years (now held at beautiful Bastyr University).

The easiest way to reach Camp Casey is via the Mukilteo-Clinton Ferry located about 45 minutes north of Seattle when traffic is reasonable. Since traffic is rarely reasonable in Seattle, 90 minutes is more realistic. Though the ferry ride itself is just 20 minutes, ferry traffic is often delayed by an hour or more. Consequently, it easily takes the better part of a day to get to Camp Casey from Seattle. Ah, but once there, the stress of the journey is quickly forgotten.

Surrounded by natural beauty, but at the same time faced with the awful job of cutting players, the last day each summer was bittersweet for me. Cutting players who put everything into making the team is one of my least favorite things about coaching.

One year, "Marty" was one such player. He loved soccer and spent much of his time playing it. In high school, he was good and his dream was to play on the team for Seattle Pacific, so he applied and the university accepted him. Prior to the start of the season, he and I talked and I was impressed with his genuine passion for the game. I liked Marty, and it seemed so did everyone who met him. He was a consummate team player, one of those "no job is too small or too big" kind of guys people love to be around. I looked forward to him competing for a spot on the team during two-a-days at Camp Casey.

During the preseason training, the assistant coaches and I assessed players on a continual basis. Sometimes it was obvious who would not make the team, other times, it was a tough decision. During our final assessment, we kept coming back to Marty. No one wanted to make the call because his passion, enthusiasm and selflessness were unmatched.

Finally, I said, "We'll give him the two o'clock game and the five o'clock ferry." That way, instead of just cutting Marty, we gave him one last memory of glory before sending him on his way.

That principle of easing a person out by giving them a moment of happiness works as well in sports as it does in an organizational management situation. I believe using compassion to help resolve heavy issues is best for all concerned.

When speaking, I share the story of "the two o'clock game and the five o'clock ferry," and often people laugh, yet that act builds solidly on the foundation of compassion.

Chinese philosopher Confucius said, "Wisdom, compassion and courage are the three universally recognized moral qualities of men." Compassion is a virtue that has me experience the world from the viewpoint of others. Compassion is the ability to feel for another human being. Cutting a player may cause heartache, disappointment and anger, so I seek to treat the player the way I would want to be treated in a similar circumstance.

I don't ever confuse compassion with weakness. If anything, being compassionate shows strength of character, strength in being secure within oneself, and strength in decisions made. Acts of authentic compassion also tend to be memorable. Former players of mine remember the lesson of that day, and many have stories of their own acts of compassion.

> *"You may call God love, you may call God goodness.*
> *But the best name for God is compassion."*

~ Meister Eckhart, German Philosopher (1260-1328)

PART II

Chapter 16
Second Chances

Winning Strategy:

Forgive quickly.

I remember my father's hands. Baseball mitts. Huge. Some fingers gnarled and one with a fingernail that never grew more than a sliver at the end of his middle finger. He was a man's man, physical in almost every sense of the word.

In the fall of 1973, I was coaching the Seattle Pacific Falcons against the University of Washington Huskies, (my friend Mike Ryan's team). As I was standing on the north sidelines of Husky Stadium, someone told me my father had been rushed to the hospital in Grand Rapids, Michigan. He was not expected to live through the night. This report came to me near the end of the game, so I saw it through to the end and then sped to the airport, booking a redeye to Grand Rapids through Chicago.

When my flight landed, I had just minutes to change planes, but I dashed to a phone and called the hospital first. That's when I heard the news that my father had died. This took away the urgency of running to catch the connecting flight, so I booked a hotel in Chicago for the night.

I made my way to the hotel, checked in, and then phoned my brother and half-sister, who gave me a full report on the situation in Michigan. We decided that I would prepare the message for our father's funeral since I was an ordained minister. I then called one of my closest friends, Paul MacVittie, to ask counsel on what to say at the funeral. Since I was told by my brother that Charles Francis McCrath committed himself to Christ four day before his death, I relayed this to MacVittie. In a heartbeat he spelled out the message I later gave at my father's funeral. The text was from 2 Timothy 4:7 in the Bible, "I have fought a good fight, I have finished my course, I have kept the faith."

I responded, "I thought that was for long distance runners (otherwise known as saints)?"

He said, "Your dad was in a fight every day of his life and albeit his course was only four days, he fulfilled the requirements."

I jotted it down on a 3" x 5" card and slept peacefully.

Most of the memories of my father I have never shared before now. He was absent for most of my childhood, but he did show up for me at a critical time when I needed him the most.

He was one of six children of a strong-willed woman and a tobacco-chewing father (a butcher by trade), neither with any patience for educating children. My father, the second youngest, was a third-grade dropout, and most of his vocabulary was profane. Even so, he was a fun one to be with except when he was drunk, (but he was funny when drunk, too.)

In my first memory of him, my brother and I are very small children. We stood on the porch awning where he put us to jump off the roof. He then caught us in front of a crowd and held us above his head by placing our feet in his enormous hands and standing us up like wooden statues. I do not remember anything but laughter. No fear.

Such was not the case when we were a little older and he took us to the back part of a sand dune and buried us side-by-side, up to our necks. I experienced my first, true, fear of death. When we both appealed to him to let us out, he acquiesced.

I did not see him for many years after that until he suddenly reentered my life when I was a teenager. At 15, I was standing before a judge with six other delinquents about to be tried and sent to reform school, which is young people prison. He was long since remarried with a new family. My mother asked him to come for me, which must have been difficult for her.

He borrowed his father's car and drove some 300 miles to appear before the judge asking to be my guardian – something he had abandoned years before. The judge allowed me to go live with my father, who was a former Detroit police officer, permanently disabled by a stabbing to the head that occurred while he was off-duty. Because of that, from the age of 29, he received a lifetime disability income, which meant he could not have another job. He started drinking.

The day we left the juvenile court, I did not know who he was or where I was going. I watched the city recede through a backseat car window, stained yellow from chewing tobacco. Eventually he said, "I'm your father. You're coming to live with me."

For the most part, I was poor (financially) throughout my early life and it was normal to wear hand-me-downs, but the year I spent with my father was the most graphic period of abject poverty. There were six of us – father, stepmother, two half-sisters, a half-brother and me in a little house down a gully, not visible from the road just above.

The house had two bedrooms, one for my two half-sisters and half-brother, the other for my dad and "Pudge" – his nickname for his wife Doreene, who weighed about 100 lbs. The kitchen was the port way to the living/dining room that served as my bedroom. I slept on a couch far too short for my six-foot frame in the only pair of long pants (not quite ankle-length) that I owned.

The sole light and heat in the house came from a Coleman lantern that hung over a linoleum clad all-purpose table. In the summer, bugs covered this table from side to side after meeting their maker sometime in the night before the flame went out.

There was no running water in the house albeit we joked there was because there was a hand pump inserted into the sink in the kitchen. This room was little more than a four-foot wide aisle that ran from the back door to a curtained area at the opposite end that served as the bathroom. The kitchen had a wood stove for cooking and an icebox that could hold a 100-pound block of ice.

However, it rarely, if ever did. My dad would fetch the ice in late afternoon, then head to the tavern in Caledonia, staying there past two a.m. By the time he came home, the ice was significantly melted (leading to frequent warm and tainted food from the icebox).

The bathroom feature was a 10-gallon pail filled with creosote that doubled as a toilet and fumigator. By the way, one of my chores was to empty the creosote pail on a pile bedecked with rats and rabbits, once each week. Looking back, I often wonder how I smelled.

By the time my father came to my rescue when I was a teenager, he was spending four to six hours per day in the tavern. When he came home, the fighting between husband and wife began. The first time I tried to break it up, he knocked me out cold for hours.

Despite the poverty and violence and my dad not working, we seemed to be happy. Most of the time. Not wanting different out of life, still I would like to have a second chance to sit with some people and do or say something other than what transpired. I'm not sure if this applies to my father or not.

What I do know is he saved me from reform school and maybe far worse. We had one gun in our gang, which was an old pirate pistol. Who can say what my life would have become without him?

His divorce from my mother was due to a combination of things. I believe these included her struggle with chronic illness (from rheumatic fever as a child), her strong will, and her becoming a Christian, which my father could not grasp, nor tolerate. Other factors that played a role included the stabbing he took to the head, and the presence of an alluring housekeeper in the home, whom he later married.

Did I grieve (wish I had known that old grief was what defined the turmoil within me)? Yes. Did I feel at times that he was a deserter? Yes. Did it lessen the love and joy I experienced when I was with him? No. Ironically, I think I fell victim to holding him as a dad-hero at times. Boys do that with their dads.

We had tons of hilarious times together in addition to some of the grave and violent times I experienced with him. He was a funny man with an engaging personality and tons of friends. When he died, his funeral was packed. I delivered the sermon at a large building in town before we went to the cemetery with his casket.

At the graveyard, I said, "Folks, there will be no lengthy eulogy here. Last week, my dad committed his life to Christ four days before he died. That means he is not in here; he is with his Heavenly Father, so please join me in the Lord's Prayer and we will repair to the reception." At that moment, I tapped the casket and said, "See you later, Dad!"

"I have fought the good fight, I have finished the race, I have kept the faith."

2 Timothy 4:7 Bible, New International Version (NIV).

Chapter 17
Dorcas

Winning Strategy:
Accountability counts.

As I mentioned, my mother took to religion and my father could not handle that. Perhaps they were fundamentally different. One way or another, well before my school years began, my mother was raising two sons as a single mother on her own.

I want to honor my mother – the single mother who was the real hero in our family. In the Bible, Dorcas is the Greek name (Tabitha is the Jewish name) of a woman beloved for her kindness to the poor, who dies from unknown causes and is brought back to life by the Apostle Peter who prays over her. Dorcas is also the name of my mother.

I had some old grief and anger due to her vision and commitment that her two sons would not grow up to be gangsters. She made sure we did not by insisting on accountability, which builds the character and essence of a successful person. Without accountability, there is failure.

As a coach, I expect accountability from my players for what they do, and perhaps even more importantly, accountability starts with me. This means owning and accepting the consequences for my actions, meeting commitments and not making excuses. Likewise, players must not blame others for negative results, poor performance or outcomes.

Dorcas did not live long enough to see all the rewards of her insistence on my accountability. She did not see me graduate college, marry my college sweetheart, earn a master's degree, become ordained, raise my children, coach national championship teams and thrive in higher education. However, her resolve was the difference between my success and failure early in life.

Dorcas gave birth to four children. The first two died shortly after birth. When my older brother Paul was born, he too was very sickly and put in an incubator for several weeks. Then I came along, a bouncing baby boy. My older brother and I lived with Dorcas and my father for a couple of years before my father left. Over the next several years, she came into and out of my life repeatedly due to health and financial issues. During her absences, she put my brother and me into the care of friends and relatives in Detroit (and for me, but not Paul, sometimes foster families.) When she came back into our lives, she guided us through the same principles and faith that guided her life. One of those principles was accountability.

We lived on Woodingham Drive near Palmer Park where my brother and I slept in a narrow bed with a v-shaped mattress resulting in two bodies being fused together as if bound by elastic bandages. Middle-of-the-night comments like "YOU'RE ON MY SIDE!" were amazing misapplications of the obvious. Later we moved to Brewster Street in Detroit, east of the Greek Market. The Brewster Roosters were the local gang.

My brother is just 14 months my senior and we fought every day, and every day I lost! Ironically, we loved each other in sort of a skewed way. We fought, but anytime I was outnumbered (or outclassed) in a fight, the first to my rescue was Paul Bernard. Our relationship – *sans* fisticuffs – continues to this day.

He faithfully calls me on February 3 to wish me a Happy Birthday, a call I return every November 25 for his birthday. Our only adult fight was when he tried a Marine Corps boot camp move on me that ended with me swinging him around in a fireman's carry. He yelled, "You're supposed to go down," and both of us ended up in unrestrained, pee-your-pants laughter.

Mom was Canadian, so we also lived from time to time in her childhood environs of Aylmer, Ontario, but most times in Detroit. We moved a lot. In that day, it was common to move before the rent was due. How and why we temporarily relocated I will never know but there were two first grades for me, perhaps due to my mother's health and economic circumstances. Thus, the second half of first grade we went to school in Canada, under the watchful eye of Dan MacGregor, the superintendent of the grade school in Aylmer.

What was missing in our lives? That's clear: a dad, money, awareness of how the rest of the world functioned, and a bed of our own. My mother's hands were weathered and tired but effective. They were worker's hands used to earn money by invisible weaving torn articles of clothing, which took a toll on her eyes.

When Dorcas placed us in the care of a foster family, she held them accountable to provide us a place to sleep and eat. That's all. She did not count on them to raise us. Consequently, as a kid with little adult supervision in my life, I was a piece of work. I continually tested the boundaries to see what I could get away with.

One of my tricks was to steal milk money that people left on their porches for dairy deliveries. I sometimes used the money I got through petty theft to buy cigarettes and booze, hanging out in pool halls and burlesque joints where I made friends with strippers and shady characters. None of this escaped Dorcas.

She seemed to know what I was doing even when she was away. Though the adults in my foster families rarely held me accountable, Dorcas did, and I was punished when I did wrong. She did not shield me. She did not accept excuses. I experienced firsthand what I have come to call the "Dorcas Principle."

I think of the Dorcas Principle often. It is a principle that avoids excuses. Though many people feel responsibility and accountability are different words for the same thing, I make a distinction between them. For me, responsibility can be shared while accountability cannot. I see being accountable as not only being responsible for something, but also being answerable for one's actions.

Proverbs 22:6 in the Bible says, "Train up a child in the way he should go; even when he is old, he will not depart from it."

Growing up in and out of foster families, I was irresponsible. Only when I lived with Dorcas, and she held me accountable for my actions, did I start to become more responsible. Had she not held me accountable even when it meant I might go to reform school, it is quite possible I may have become a world-class gangster or criminal instead of a world-class soccer coach.

Chapter 18
Bev Jacques

Winning Strategy:
Take an interest in the people around you.

Bev, so named because his mother wanted a girl, was the chain-smoking, owner (? – maybe operator) of the local pool hall. This was a main-street establishment located on the second floor above a grocery store (where I later bagged potatoes and stacked shelves). Working downstairs in the grocery store as a teenager, I discovered I could peek up women's dresses when they walked across the grates in the store's aisles above.

The beauty of Bev's pool hall was access via a rear stairway, which allowed more clandestine entry, inasmuch as pool halls were lumped together with taverns and brothels (whorehouses) as dens of iniquity. Of course, for me and my pals, any appearances in Bev's place presupposed truancy from school. This was a fact Bev did not seem to view as criminal, which may explain why he never mentioned it, freeing me for lifetime learning degrees still in place today.

One of the more popular and lucrative subjects was a game called 101, played on billiard tables, which are much larger than eight ball tables. The game featured 15 unnumbered yellow billiard balls and one white cue ball. The pockets were numbered and a leather flask provided each player with a numbered "pea" secretly pocketed before the first shot was taken. (The most prized pea was #16 requiring only 85 points to win.) This game provided tons of life lessons caringly taught by Bev, such as "how to keep a secret," and "how to steal and deceive within the confines of a game rather than in real life." This was akin to stealing second base in baseball.

We also learned about not belittling or minimizing others due to any limitations or inabilities. For example, no one – make that NO ONE EVER asked Bev about his name. It became perfectly clear that any reference to Bev never included inquiries about how he got his name!

Bev also taught us tricks – still in use – about how to catch baseballs and footballs, how to shoot a puck, how to pitch horseshoes and, one of my life favorites: How to throw any kind of ball or object high above our heads and catch it behind our backs. Every time. Without failure. (I can still do it today!)

Bev, also, was a walking compendium of life wisdom and wise counsel. I remember going to him one time with my dream of playing hockey in the NHL. He said, "Come back and see me after you have skated 10,000 hours!"

"That's it?" I asked.

He didn't respond.

Bev was of slight stature and bowlegged, measuring not much more than five feet four inches tall, but he was a giant to all of us. Still is.

Bev Jacques took an interest in people with a genuine openness that involved caring and listening. It's easier said than done, but taking an interest in others is a very important trait for a good coach to develop.

Chapter 19
Revival for Survival

Winning Strategy:
Show up and be coachable.

A lightning bolt realization hit me as a teenager on the evening of June 22, 1954. It was a Tuesday night on Kalamazoo Avenue in Grand Rapids, Michigan, and an old-fashioned tent meeting went up in town near a cemetery. This revival featured Dr. Bob Wells, a fire-balling evangelical preacher from Bob Jones University in South Carolina.

How I came to be there on a summer evening involved the girl I wanted to marry, a dark-haired beauty named Sue. She was a cheerleader who would not go to the places I sought entertainment, so I searched for one she valued. When we saw the sign "Revival for Survival," we made plans to attend.

At the end of the fireballer's message, which I am convinced he created after an FBI search of my life, he asked those who were "guilty" to come to the front. In a sawdust-strewn area behind the platform, the fireballer and his choir performed their magic.

I was seated across a card table from a young, athletic looking man who I came to know only as Al. He began asking me what my dreams and thoughts were about my future life. He did not point his finger to tell me how bad I was, a familiar exercise I had experienced with other Christians.

I found myself sharing far more personal secrets than ever before. At some point, he spoke, and this is when the lightning struck.

"Everything you wish for," he said, "and want to be, you can achieve if you put your faith in Jesus Christ."

(Faith, whatever that is, I thought. Moreover, Christ, whoever that is -- whose name I regularly took in vain about every five words.)

There are many sidebars to what happened next, but the fact is I did so (put my faith in Christ) that night. Approximately two weeks later, another lightning bolt hit when I looked at the untouched pack of Red and White Pall Mall cigarettes. I knew something had changed in me. Prior to my meeting with Al a fortnight before, I smoked two packs each day. After the lightning subsided, another bolt hit when I realized I no longer profaned the name of Jesus Christ. That was 64 years ago and still counting.

Later that summer, Sue enrolled in Hope College in Holland, Michigan – a school founded by Dutch pioneers and affiliated with the Reformed Church, while I headed to Wheaton, citadel of evangelical Christianity. I came out of the gates as a new Christian fireball for Christ myself. God was my guide and the author and finisher of my faith.

Then I started to doubt. Satan started to creep in.

My second year on campus, I sat down with Major Ian Thomas, an evangelist from England invited to conduct a week of special meetings at Wheaton. Major Thomas, the founder of Torchbearers International (in 1947), was also available for one-to-one counseling. This was a big moment for me.

He said to me, "Salvation is like this. You are walking, and Jesus taps you and says, 'follow me.' You become a child of God through a process called conversion."

From that point on, the journey in sanctification begins, he explained. Thomas defined sanctification as "the process of becoming what God called you to become the minute you trusted in Christ."

Sixty years later, I still find that explanation of sanctification is the best. God's son paid the ultimate price so that our names could be written in the Book of Life the moment of belief. That took away my mental anguish. We are already declared the finished product.

The business of staying in a higher discipline as a Christian is more difficult, and to testify to strangers went against my grain. Thomas had the same experience and felt guilty all the time. He told me a story from his own life.

In those days, the seats on an airplane were not pre-assigned. He thought he had to testify every time he was on a plane, and he didn't know how to go about it. He came to reckon with this by praying just before the flight, "Lord, I'm available if you need me." Then he would find the best seat on the plane and sit down. If anyone sat beside him, he knew they had been placed next to him for a purpose.

My meeting with him afforded me the chance to confide some major doubts I was experiencing in my new life as a Christian. He shared insights and experiences of his own, and here are some of his foundation messages used to this day for Torchbearers International:

"As a young evangelist, my love and enthusiasm for Christ as my Saviour kept me very, very busy until out of sheer frustration, I finally came to the point

of quitting. That was the turning point which transformed my Christian life. In my despair I discovered that the Lord Jesus gave Himself FOR me, so that risen from the dead He might give Himself TO me, He who IS the Christian Life. Instead of pleading for help I began to thank Him for all that He wanted to be, sharing His Life with me every moment of every day. I learned to say "Lord Jesus, I can't, You never said I could; but You can, and always said You would. That is all I need to know". From that moment life became the adventure that God always intended it to be." ~Major W. Ian Thomas

Prior to meeting with Major Thomas, as a new Christian, I tried not to sin. I also attempted to read and memorize the entire Bible. What I learned in my failure to do either is that what I needed was to admit I did not have all the answers.

Being coachable is an attitude. It applies to sports, business, parenting, spiritual lessons, and even to old coaches themselves. It involves being willing to learn new things, being open to change, and having a desire for personal growth.

Coachable people grow, learn and find success. It is the secret to achieving dreams.

Chapter 20
Michigan

Winning Strategy:

Let the past be your teacher.

The Michigan chapter of my life covers a whole lot of ground. It was the site of my birth, early years, teen years and many stops and drop-ins along the way since then. My heart is still there and my mind races back on a regular basis when triggered by memories, or calls from friends and family. I also do frequent check-ins on the progress of the Lions, Tigers and Redwings. (The Pistons, however, not so much.)

It was 5:58 a.m. on Feb 3, 1936, that Charles Clifford McCrath was extracted from Dorcas Jane Baxter McCrath's womb, thus beginning my journey in the human corridor. It's too bad one-minute-old babies can't reason and talk, for if that were possible C. Clifford would have waxed eloquent about what it was like to spend several months listening to conversations between Chuck and Dorcas. That would have been spliced with frequent babbles, gibberish and laughter from older brother (née November 25, 1934) Paul Bernard McCrath who was the third child of the couple to be born and the first to survive.

Dorcas, a very beautiful woman, was plagued with a litany of maladies including a badly damaged heart from a childhood fever, and leukemia. The early years in Detroit were speckled with an endless parade of highs and lows, what adults might rue as a mixture of curse and blessing.

She met Chuck (my father) after befriending his sister, my aunt Charity, who worked as a clerk at J.L. Hudson's in downtown Detroit. The J.L. Hudson Building was a department store located at 1206 Woodward Avenue, and construction began in 1911, with additions throughout the years until completion in 1946. The name came from the company's founder, Joseph Lowthian Hudson.

Charity embraced Dorcas, an "escapee" from a bad marriage in Aylmer, Ontario, Canada, some 120 miles east and a few miles north of Lake Erie. She told her about her younger brother and the match was on. Chuck

(Charles Francis McCrath) journeyed to Detroit from Grand Rapids, Michigan, where he and Charity grew up.

Chuck and Charity were two of the six children of Walter (b.1873) and Louise (Rathbun) McCrath (b. 1879), who lived on Burton Street. I later lived there, too, the summer after high school before heading to Wheaton College. Grandpa Walt was a tobacco-chewing butcher by trade, and I picture him sitting beside an antique Zenith radio in an even older rocking chair, spitting tobacco into a Maxwell House coffee can. Walt and Louise would have upstaged Lucy and Desi had TV been invented.

One unforgettable day, Walt forked his way into the first bite of Grandma Lou's roast, and grumbled, "Meat's tough."

In a flash, Grandma Lou shot back, "TOUGHER WHERE THERE AIN'T ANY!"

Walt outlived Louise by several years (she died in 1957 and he passed away in 1965). They are buried side-by-side in Oak Grove Cemetery on Kalamazoo Avenue in Grand Rapids.

My Michigan past defines me and this stretch of my history includes never-to-be-forgotten experiences under the heading "Why am I still alive today?"

Soon after my parents divorced, and Dorcas was raising two young sons as a single mother, she took a job as an LPN at the Henry Ford Hospital. One day, my brother Paul and I were "hiding out" in a building incinerator when we decided to set a match to the cardboard contents. Cardboard, by the way, happens to burn white hot and far quicker than paper. About this time, Dorcas was walking along the adjacent alley, which was how she traveled to and from work. Paul cried out to her, and she ran to the rapidly heating inferno, managing to extract us from what would have been a ghastly death.

Then there was the time I scaled the skeleton of a five-story munitions building. High above the earth, I walked around the perimeter of the top story of the unfinished building. Just as I was doing this, Dorcas stepped off a bus on the street below and I shouted from five floors up, "Hey Mom!" which I'm sure withdrew several year's deposits from her life on the planet.

On another occasion, my snowsuit belt caught the back door handle, propelling me out of the car as Dorcas, who was driving, rounded a corner. This was just long enough to throw me under the vehicle. A man standing on the corner waiting for a streetcar ran after us yelling for Dorcas to stop, or there would be no Uncle Nubby today.

He gathered me up and minutes later, I was on the top floor of a very high building where a doctor painted my body with iodine using a three-inch wide paintbrush. My screams could be heard across the Detroit River and throughout Canada, or so I was told.

Experience is the best teacher we have and a great reminder of our vast capabilities to face whatever life brings. Storytelling increases resilience when navigating tough times, and connecting with people through personal stories is one of the less known, but most significant ways of becoming a better coach, and friend.

Chapter 21
The Gump

Winning Strategy:
Joy is powerful.

Of all the "goodbyes" in my life, not all were sad affairs. One that was joyful (make that hilarious) was the farewell to the Gump, my 1947 four-door Nash Rambler. I drove the car 200 miles to Wheaton College only to sell it within the next year.

Like many vehicles in those days, it had soft pistons, which led to high oil consumption and nauseating belches of acrid, blue smoke emanating from the exhaust pipe. I asked an artist to paint on the trunk of the car in old English text "The GUMP!"

I bought it for $100, but after buffing it to a deep, navy shine, it was beautiful from the outside and I sold it for $200. Maybe because the Gump felt betrayed, he soon began to deteriorate and, legend has it, the car changed hands many times. After numerous citations for illegal parking, and abandoning a vehicle, local police confiscated the vehicle. Since we never followed the standard procedures for changing ownership, they soon tracked me down as the rightful owner.

The Gump became notorious and well known by everybody on campus. In any event, to get the Gump back there was an inordinate fee that had to be paid. Clearly, I did not have the funds to do so, which resulted in a summons to trial.

As it turned out, the trial was on the docket for night court where the Gump was listed with a variety of classic night court cases including prostitution, petty theft, sidewalk drunks, etc., etc. Word got around that the Gump was on trial, and by the time night court convened, there were in excess of 90 fellow students with me in the courtroom.

The judge entered, dressed in a shabby, brown plaid suit with a yellowing, wrinkled shirt and an unmatched tie that would bring tears to a comedian's eyes. He was a diminutive man with a rather large, bald head, and a worrisome sort of scalp disease. While listening to the charges he persistently scratched his scalp sending dandruff-like flakes descending on his paperwork.

After dispatching with three or four of the first cases, the judge caroled, "Next case?"

The responsible officer said, "Your honor it's the Gump again!"

At this, the judge bolted straight up in his chair, "Oh no, not the Gump!" he cried.

The facts were presented including frequent abandonment and angry calls from citizens (complaining about the Gump on their front lawns), together with my confirming ownership, but inability to pay. I was a poor college student working nights in a publishing company for minimum wage, which at that time was $.85 per hour.

There were many tearful (heh heh) testimonies from students who avowed that the Gump had changed their lives or, at the very least had given them hope to continue living. After listening, and pounds more dandruff, the judge stated he was prepared to provide his ruling.

"Guilty, of all charges," he said.

To everyone's shock and dismay, the judge not only declared the Gump guilty, he also sentenced him to death! If it were today, protestors would still be rallying, but at that time, it appeared to be a humane and caring judgment.

The goodbye came the following Thursday at Wheaton, during the time for chapel, a short mandatory service on campus that began at 10:30 and ended at 11 a.m. daily. All students, faculty, and staff were required to attend, but the day of the Gump's demise, 14 of us skipped chapel.

We pushed the Gump from a side street on campus to the middle of the inner walkway, which also served as a motorway for maintenance vehicles. Then, 12 "pallbearers" stood by ready to pull the Gump from Pierce Chapel to Corey Gymnasium, where a towing company waited to carry the offender away. With two ropes tied to the bumpers (the Gump Bumps), six to a side tugged the Gump forward just as Pierce Chapel belched its inhabitants to the street.

Sitting regally in the back seat of the Gump, dressed in tuxedo and stovepipe hat, was Johnny O'Neal, Wheaton's 157-pound wrestler (and soon-to-be the national champion). Hiding in the front, squeezed under the dashboard, I steered the Gump forward while Johnny gave driving directions through the funeral procession.

Soon 2,000 students, staff and even the college president hailed, cheered and joyfully lamented the Gump's last mile! Once at Corey Gymnasium, the pallbearers served as chauffeurs, opening the door for Sir John and helping extract me from beneath the dashboard. Alas, as the Gump inched up the ramp of the tow truck, we place our hands over hearts, and bid our fond farewell...the last GOODBYE to the Gump!

Chapter 22
Wheaton

Winning Strategy:

"May You Live All the Days of Your Life"
~Jonathan Swift, 1667-1745

Wheaton College in Illinois was founded by evangelical abolitionists in 1860, and according to the Princeton Review, "Wheaton is arguably the best school in the nation with a Christ-based worldview." I was blessed in many ways to attend Wheaton, where I met lifelong friends and the future mother of my children.

Midge ran with a wealthy crowd and her dad said she needed to finish school before we married. Her childhood began in Portland, Oregon, but her family moved often with her father's promotions. He was a career executive for the multimillion-dollar American Can Co. (the only employer he ever knew). Wheaton was an obvious choice for college for Midge since by that time, her family lived in nearby Park Ridge, Illinois. Later, they moved to Stamford, Connecticut. She was raised in a much more reserved fashion than my more or less street kid free-range upbringing on the streets of Detroit.

The first time she saw me, I was dressed as a female clown wearing gobs of lipstick and a basketball uniform with two basketballs stuffed in my shirt. I was the third man on top of two others pitched into her high school swimming pool in front of 200 Young Life club members.

One year later, our eyes met in a crowd. She was a freshman at Wheaton and I was a junior emceeing a new student orientation event for Big Brothers/Big Sisters. At that time, I was doing a great deal of speaking and spent five hours a week writing humor. She moved with a sophisticated grace, perhaps unaware of the male eyes following her very attractive figure through the room.

We met during the mingling part of the event, replete with cookies and juice. She was 18 and the spitting image of Elizabeth Taylor, the young, dark-haired beauty starring in the movie *Giant* with James Dean. I stopped and looked at Midge, and I just stared.

I did not see her again for nearly two years. By then I had graduated and was coaching the Wheaton men's soccer team, but I was still eating my meals in the school cafeteria. It was a warm spring evening, the last day of

April in 1958, when our paths next crossed. I was walking up the steps to the cafeteria just as she was walking down the steps.

She wore a beautiful yellow summer dress and held a glass of grape juice in her hand. The moment stabbed me, churning up emotions of wonder and confusion. We both stopped, and stared eye-to-eye once again. Perhaps it was my intensity that stopped her in her tracks. She was more of a woman now than when we first met. All reality faded away to a low murmur of voices through the doors beyond the steps.

There was an Ogden Nash event on campus that night sponsored by the Wheaton College Student Union. Nash was the most famous American poet of light and humorous verse, and he was touring the country. Most speakers invited to campus were serious, so this was to be a very unusual event at Pierce Chapel that very evening.

"Would you like to go?"

"Yes," she said with excitement, then promptly spilled the juice on her dress.

The event began at 8:30 p.m. and admission was $1.

It was the buzz of the campus that I invited Midge that day and we went to see Ogden Nash that night. Officially, Wheaton rules required asking the girl's dorm mother one week in advance for permission for a date. Perhaps since it was Ogden Nash, and we were going to the chapel on campus, we tiptoed around the rules.

We married two days before her graduation on June 11, 1960, in Park Ridge, Illinois. My aunt came, and my brother was best man. (My mother passed away four years earlier, so she was not there.) Then Midge and I began our amazing journey together, traveling to the East Coast.

Our destination was Gordon College, 25 miles from Boston, and three miles from the ocean in Wenham, Massachusetts, on Boston's North Shore. This was to be my second college coaching post, since Wheaton was the first. I wore many different hats on campus, from public relations director to interim dean, and taught science at nearby Brookwood School in Manchester. Our first child, our daughter Stacey, was born while we were living in Massachusetts.

After six years, an opportunity came to return to my home state of Michigan for a new coaching position. Midge and I prayed about whether we should go. We visited the campus together and made our decision. Our son Steve was born while we were in Michigan, where I was the men's soccer coach and dean of students for Spring Arbor College.

Just a few years later, we faced another choice and it was not an easy decision to leave Spring Arbor for yet another school, 2,000 miles away. We were very happy in Michigan. Again, we prayed about it and decided we would go to Seattle Pacific College in Washington. Seattle is where we both live to this day, nearly 50 years later.

However, after more than 25 years of marriage, my Wheaton College sweetheart and I were living parallel lives. I was gone 150 days a year and Midge was very busy as a federal program teacher and other responsibilities, such as her women's group "Just Friends," which met at our house (the kids called the group "Just Enemies" because they had to stay in their rooms).

Eventually she thought a separation would help, so I moved downstairs. She then wanted a real separation, so I moved out. At that point, I was still mowing the lawn. There were six months of meetings, all very spiritual, then the D word. It was 1986 and our children were by then in college. I must say, it was the most beautiful divorce in the history of divorce. Ultimately, the beauty of our union is our two children Stacey and Steve and our grandchildren: Keith (K.C.), Stephen (Stevie), Kieran and Sienna. This book is dedicated to them.

In my reflection on the early days at Wheaton, the friends met and kept, and the trials of love and marriage, we lived triumphantly.

Dreams do exact a price, though, and it is possible the cost of my career as a traveling collegiate coach was not spending as much time as I would have liked at home with my family. The past is not something that can be changed, but with experience comes wisdom.

As for Ogden Nash, he was not known for being a religious man, though he was a member of the Episcopal congregation of St. Andrews-by-the-Sea in New Hampshire. He died in 1971 and a poem of his was read at his funeral.

I Didn't Go To Church Today

I didn't go to church today,

I trust the Lord to understand.

The surf was swirling blue and white,

The children swirling on the sand.

He knows, He knows how brief my stay,

How brief this spell of summer weather,

He knows when I am said and done,

We'll have plenty of time together.

~Ogden Nash.

Chapter 23
Camp Brookwoods

Winning Strategy:
Do your job with flexibility, not "flubbability."

It was my junior year at Wheaton College when one of my six housemates, Bob "Whitey" Whitehead, announced to me that we were "going to camp this summer!"

"*Au contraire*," I said.

Camp, from my wayward youth until that moment, always implied detention as punishment for various missteps. Nonetheless, within the next few minutes we headed to the "Stupe" to keep the appointment Whitey set.

The Stupe was the nickname for the campus student union where students passed time when they should have been studying. At the Stupe, we took our seats across the table from a handsome, middle-aged man named Miles Strodel.

Miles was a Wheaton graduate who was the headmaster of Lexington Christian Academy in Massachusetts. During the summer months, he was the director of Camp Sandy Hill located on the west bank of the East River in North East, Maryland, a small town on the Chesapeake Bay.

He was a peaceful looking man with the word "disciplined" engraved somewhere within his soul or just inside his forehead, which would surely be revealed in an autopsy performed after his demise. However, the indelible feature of Miles, etched in my mind forever, I discovered when he extended his right hand with fingers that were curled toward his palm.

Immediately, it was apparent that his right arm was significantly shriveled, dwarfed by a muscular, and well-developed left arm and left hand the size of a baseball glove. Later revelations proved even more amazing when I learned that upon graduation from Wheaton, he was invited to the Chicago Cubs baseball team training camp. (Three-fingered Mordecai Brown made it to the major leagues as a pitcher and, after a stunning career, was inducted into the baseball Hall of Fame. It is a safe bet that Miles, who batted left-handed, might have become a great slugger.)

Aside from his athletic ability, Miles had a calling from God to teach in a Christian environment. Consequently, he moved to Boston where he eventually took the posts at Lexington Christian Academy and Camp Sandy Hill. It didn't take long before Whitey and I succumbed to Miles' persuasive powers and signed on as Sandy Hill staff members for the summer of 1957.

After the first year, for the next 13 summers, I was assigned to Brookwoods Wilderness Adventure in New Hampshire, founded by a Boston City radiologist, Dr. Lawrence Andreson, also a Wheaton graduate. He purchased land on the shores of Lake Winnipesaukee near Alton, New Hampshire, and it is still a Christian youth summer camp to the present day.

He envisioned a healthy alternative for young people (he had two sons and a daughter) that became Camp Brookwoods, which is celebrating its 75th anniversary in 2019. Inasmuch as Miles was the headmaster of Lexington Christian Academy, Doc A. approached him to lead the program beginning in the summer of 1958. Miles, in keeping with his strong, ethical beliefs, notified the entire Sandy Hill staff that he accepted the position at Camp Brookwoods and would not be returning to Sandy Hill in 1958. It is no surprise that 95 percent of the staff followed him to New Hampshire. Thus began one of the most significant, life-changing chapters in my life.

The dawn at Brookwoods brought with it the kind of energy and excitement that only a couple days of fasting can provide. Miles (and his marvelous wife, "Aunt Gracie") were there to welcome me my first day and see me escorted to Bear Cabin, which would become my summer home for the next several summers. It housed 12 campers who I would shepherd as my brood.

In addition, I directed several of the sports. This included roles as soccer instructor, basketball coach, waterfront teacher for waterskiing, and NRA rifle trainer. I was also the program director responsible for the evening programs every night of the nine weeks of camp.

Each summer there were two camp periods of one month each. Between these sessions, there was a one-week period during which time we had approximately 100 boys who were wards of the courts. They came to Camp Brookwoods from the Boston juvenile division. Naturally, I was right at home with these guys.

Among the takeaways from my years at Brookwoods are a lifetime of friendships, including Paul MacVittie, who later captained my first soccer team at Gordon College, and JJ Thomassian, a shop teacher from Kew Gardens, in Queens, New York. JJ's approach to pancakes is the same way I eat pancakes to this very day. He stacks the pancakes, pours syrup, carves one-inch squares with a knife, and then spears a stacked bite with his fork, putting a bite in his mouth, very neat, like an art form. He and his wife Rose are my lifelong friends and my hardest laughter in life, I experienced with JJ during my visit with him in Kew Gardens one Christmas in the 1960s.

Miles Strodel and Woody (Sherwood) Strodel, a taller, somewhat string-beanish younger brother of Miles, were an inspiration to all. Woody went on to become the youth pastor in several prestigious churches including historic Park Street Church on the Boston Commons, where gunpowder was stored in the basement during the Revolutionary War. He married his wife Dawn, the love his life, who he met at Gordon College in Boston. Camp Brookwoods was part of their youth ministry that also took them to Coral Springs Presbyterian Church and the famed Highland Park Presbyterian Church in Dallas, Texas.

At Camp Brookwoods, Woody was the staff leader and a master of slogans that had no connection to proper English but remain ingrained in my mind to this day. A couple: "Do your job with flexibility, but not flubability!" And to help encourage when the going got tough: "The first 100 years are the hardest!"

I served as program director and all-round comedian at Camp Brookwoods, and to this day, consider it my best job of all. This is where I was responsible for creating every evening's special program, which included skit night and where the famous Story of the Nub originated. (Most people call me Nubber, and at Northwest Soccer Camp, Uncle Nubby...where I am still doing my job with flexibility, not flubbability.)

Chapter 24
Head Wall

Winning Strategy:
Accept help when needed.

At Camp Brookwoods, once a week staff received a one-day break from camp, albeit, it was just the daylight segment of a given day. On one of these free days in August, my friend Paul MacVittie (my soul mate pal) and I decided to climb nearby Mt. Washington in the White Mountains of New Hampshire.

The mountain is 6,288 feet high at the summit, and a popular climb, though sometimes very dangerous due to weather. The Huntington Trail above the timberline is the mountain's most treacherous path, replete with foreboding warning signs. These harbingers of doom discourage further passage for all but the most skilled climbers. One warning read: "Beyond this point are some of the most dangerous winds in the world – some gusts measuring over 200 miles per hour!" Another: "More people have died beyond this point than in 90 percent of the mountains in the world!"

However, for two, red-blooded, invincible punks from the back alleys of America, no such omens stood a chance. It was about 80 degrees and uncommonly humid the day we arrived, and the parking area at the base of the mountain looked like the tailgating area of any ballpark.

The two of us, in Bermuda shorts and T-shirts, tied jackets around our wastes and began hop, stepping and bounding across house-sized boulders bordering the parking lot. In a way, these giant rocks served as sentinels of safe climbing by making it somewhat difficult to access the entrance to the base camp for the Huntington Trail. We chatted, laughed, farted, and reviled the timid souls who elected to climb near the Cog Railway adjacent to the paved roadway. The "non-climbers" used that path for safe and quick access to the Summit House.

Come what may, we chose the more difficult route. It wasn't long before we encountered two scrubby looking, bearded (hippy-like) "woodsmen" descending rather carefully. They seemed far more weathered than the two of us and did not speak, though they seemed very interested in scrutinizing and assessing us as if looking at mannequins in a window.

We would see them again.

Had we any notion of the danger on ahead, we would have taken the job of keeping ourselves alive much more seriously. Although it was a warm summer day when we parked, Mt. Washington's rapidly changing weather claims a steady count of victims. Most tourists (and sane people) opt for the aforementioned Cog Railway to reach the summit. It's a pleasant, scenic train ride to the highest peak in the Northeast, and for those in vehicles, a motorway runs parallel to the railway for easy access.

The Huntington Trail, by contrast, abuts a stream cascading from somewhere near the summit down past the parking areas and eventually out to the Atlantic Ocean. There are several streams emanating from the White Mountains that pick-up steam as they head to the sea. One is the Saco River that runs through New Hampshire and Maine, on which I led wilderness campers over dangerous white water and falls requiring portaging at several junctures.

Yet, I digress. We left the parking lot that late summer day of 1958 clad in hiking shorts with soccer-style jerseys wrapped like cummerbunds around our waists. The early part of our journey began by crossing the Texas-sized boulders abutting both sides of a stream (that eventually unites with other White Mountain streams to form more robust waterways). We had not climbed far before meeting (the aforementioned) pair of bearded, scruffy-looking guys looking like best-supporting actors in the film *Deliverance* (though that movie came out in 1972, some years later). They eyed us like bait for later trappings.

So far, so good, but the first indication that there might be something wrong was a chill that began creeping into our previously warm and sweaty bodies. Within a few minutes, we unstrapped the jerseys serving as waistbands and donned them to help buffer the cold. To make matters worse, the sky darkened, and a wind picked up bringing with it a few drops of rain.

We continued to climb with neither of us daring to acknowledge the somewhat drastic change in air temperature. We now had reached the last thin layer of the tree line affording us a panoramic view of the summit as well as the infamous and foreboding southeast face wall of Tuckerman's Ravine. Then it happened. The drops of rain became a torrential downpour forcing us to seek shelter, which was nonexistent. The trees, now far behind us, ruled out any thought of retreat. Shivering, we huddled together and actually prayed aloud for some sort of rescue.

The rain abated briefly allowing us to forge ahead wet, but with renewed confidence that we were not that far from the Summit House. How wrong we were. It seemed like a lifetime of additional climbing when we came face-to-face with what every novice Mt. Washington climber knows about the Huntington Trail to the top: THE HEAD WALL! The head wall is a 30-feet high, 30-yards wide buttress that must be scaled with proper climbing equipment in order to continue to the Summit House.

There is no way around it. Up and over is the only option. By then, the temperature had dropped to the 30s and the wind was swirling so violently we could hardly hear each other talk. Our teeth chattered, and our bodies went numb with cold. We were in deep trouble. Tuckerman's Ravine in the Presidential Range of the White Mountains has a long history of traumatic deaths from hypothermia and accidents, though we did not know that at the time.

Suddenly, as if dropped from the sky, the hippy woodsmen reappeared, last seen what seemed like eons ago at the trailhead. They came to our rescue bedecked in ropes, hatchet-like pitons, and Appalachian Club climbing equipment just as every extremity of our bodies and our minds were freezing. They explained that the way we were dressed (or, in our case, not dressed) showed the telltale signs of perfect candidates for rescue. They also told us that two weeks earlier, at this very same spot, an MIT student and his fiancée died of hypothermia. (Paul Zanet and Judy March died of exposure and exhaustion on July 19, 1958. They were dressed in light summer clothing, as we were.)

We stood in disbelief, putty in their hands to do anything they decreed. They roped us up and one of the two angels scaled the wall to form the upper end of the tandem that would pull us up. Before the ascent, they warned that the moment we surfaced above the wall to make sure to remain prone. They clarified that the wind was in excess of 100 miles per hour with gusts upwards of 180! Impossible, I thought to myself, and during the ordeal managed to forget the warning. I was the first rise dragged over the crown of the wall, and suddenly feeling more invincible, stood up. In an instant, the wind knocked me facedown.

MacVittie was next, and I greeted him with shouts of, "Stay down!" The other mountain climber followed and soon we all traversed the final 200 yards to the Summit House, where we could warm ourselves with hot coffee by a blazing fire. The last 50 yards, I turned around and walked backwards, leaning back with my body inches from the ground, buoyed by the same wind that was our potential demise. The backwards walk was the first indication that we were not going to die and could laugh a bit at our plight. Soon, we found ourselves huddling around a potbellied stove surrounded by scores of people who had no clue how close they were to what easily could have been two frozen corpses. Later, we took the Cog Rail back to the parking lot and no longer feigned bravado.

Chapter 25
Gordon College

Winning Strategy:
Invest in yourself.

After Wheaton, the "real stuff" came in 1960 when Midge and I headed to

Gordon College in Boston, where I became head coach of the school's new

soccer team. The school had recently decided to replace football with soccer.

Hal Murdoch, who hired me for the job, heard of me through Dick

Camp, one of my two best pals at Wheaton. Dick, a minister's son from Fair

Lawn, New Jersey, was an All-American Athlete in football. After graduation

from Wheaton, he headed to Gordon Divinity School (now Gordon-Conwell

Theological Seminary) where he became good friends with Murdoch, the

athletic director and basketball coach. The two played one-on-one basketball

at noon each day in an old polo barn with a roof so low they had to learn to

shoot flat shots.

One day while they played basketball, Murdoch told my old friend that Gordon needed a soccer coach.

"I've got the guy for you!" Dick said. POW!

At that time, Gordon was so small (less than 400 students), it had little money to offer. This led to a compensation package that included free housing in one of the new dormitories for 28 men, mostly freshmen.

Midge and I were newlyweds in our early 20s when we unpacked our belongings into the little one-room apartment in the men's dorm. This is where we lived the entire seven years at Gordon. The small size of the school meant that within one year I had nine jobs. This included soccer coach, hockey coach, house parent, director of housing, director of student procurement (a title I argued with great intensity), communications teacher, and assistant director of public relations. I was also the school bus driver for practice teachers and had a side job chopping wood on the Merrill Estate for the widow heiress of the Merrill Lynch fortune.

There were three other jobs I did in Massachusetts at the same time. I taught science at nearby Brookwood School in Manchester (not to be confused with Brookwoods Camp in New Hampshire!). Midge, the best teacher on the planet, then and now, outlined nightly what I waxed eloquent about the following day. I also led the after-school recreation program at Shore Country Day School in Beverly. Then on the weekends, Midge and I traveled into Boston to lead a youth group at Boston's famous Park Street Church. We drove from Gordon College to the Park Street Church in Boston three times every weekend for four years, which were some of the best days of our lives.

Adjacent to the Park Street Church is the city's third-oldest burial ground, established in 1660, which is the final resting place of Paul Revere, of midnight ride fame. The corner of Park and Tremont faces the Boston Common and is just a short block down the hill from the Massachusetts State House, the golden domed state capitol building. In 1960, the year we arrived, John F. Kennedy was the junior U.S. Senator from Massachusetts (which he resigned in December 1960 to become the 35th President of the United States.)

At Gordon, Paul MacVittie (my Mt. Washington hiking partner) was the first guy on the soccer team and I made him captain. He was an all-sports guy, and perhaps people didn't know of his true brilliance. After Gordon, he went on to earn a PhD at Fuller Theological Seminary and he's now a clinical psychologist in New Hampshire. Though we live on opposite sides of the country, we still talk constantly and have been joined at the hip for years. Dr. Paul MacVittie's youngest of three sons, Major William MacVittie, is a U.S.

Air Force officer and flight commander, who completed multiple deployments in Iraq and Afghanistan.

At Gordon, I was the acting dean of students until the Harvard-educated Dr. William "Bill" Worden accepted the post as first dean. Although he was a thoroughgoing non-jock, we became fast friends after our first offspring were born two days apart. Stacey was born on Friday the 13th of December. Bill and Pat's son Michael was born two days later, on Sunday, December 15, 1963, which resulted in the two of us bonding in a tremendous way.

That weekend, while both mamas were still in the hospital, the two of us, well outside the boundaries of Gordon College's restrictions, enjoyed steak and baked potatoes topped off with cigars. (Smoking in restaurants was allowed in the '60s.) We also had brandy (or was it cognac?). In any event, we stayed well attached for the next few years, during which time, with some worldly help from me, he authored a book entitled *PDA*, which stood for *Personal Death Awareness*.

Writing the book involved numerous interviews and one of the areas of research was labeled "living autopsies," wherein he would conduct interviews with those who failed at their attempts to kill themselves. Worden's lifelong research included interviews with prisoners of war, at least one of whom, General William Dean, tried to commit suicide.

While on the subject of death, I never wanted any players to pre-decease me, but Joey Welker, who played on my team at Gordon College, was shot down in Vietnam on October 11, 1967. Lieutenant Abram Joseph Welker was 23 years old. Others who died before their time include Bill Scofield from Spring Arbor College, and Steve Newman and Dennis Kain on my early teams at Seattle Pacific.

My time at Gordon prepared me to help others in times of grief (and celebrations of life). While coaching at Gordon College, I studied theology in the then campus divinity school, and became an ordained minister. Homiletics is the art of preaching, and I remember one particular lesson as if it were this morning. For this class, each student had to prepare and deliver a 10-minute sermon.

"Now Brother McCrath," creaked Reverend Dr. Lloyd Perry, who was badly twisted up physically from being hit by a car. "How do we get a noun in the plural?"

Dr. Perry's career spanned five decades and six colleges, he preached throughout the United States, and wrote 24 books on the subjects of preaching and the Bible. No detail escaped him. According to Dr. Perry, three nouns in the plural are all that people can stand in a 30-minute sermon. He also believed there should be one hour of preparation for each minute of sermon delivered. Another big thing for him was alliteration.

This was my 10-minute sermon: <u>Rejoice, Refrain, Rely, Relax.</u>

The four R's of my 1960s sermonette come from Philippians 4:4-7 in the Bible.

[4] Rejoice in the Lord always: and again, I say, Rejoice.

[5] Let your moderation be known unto all men. The Lord is at hand.

[6] Be careful for nothing; but in everything by prayer and supplication with thanksgiving let your requests be made known unto God.

[7] And the peace of God, which passeth all understanding, shall keep your hearts and minds through Christ Jesus.

I explained it to the class in the following way:

(Rejoice) in the Lord always.

Let your moderation be evident to all. (Refrain.)

Let your requests be made known to God. (Rely.)

And the Peace of God, which transcends all understanding, will guard your hearts and your minds in Christ Jesus. (Relax.)

Dr. Perry cleared his throat and his voice still echoes in my mind.

"Now my brothers what's the noun?" he asked. "It's admonition."

I could see what was coming.

"Brother McCrath, let's look at the result of those admonitions. Now my brothers, rejoice, refrain, rely, relax. How do we get a noun in the plural?"

Well, apparently, according to Dr. Perry, "relax" in not an admonition. The peace of God is a result of faith. It is not an admonition, which is the gentle counsel or reproof that describes the first three R's (rejoice, refrain, and rely).

Dr. Perry was one of the most fascinating professors in my long career as a student and even longer one in college administration. A coach is in many ways a teacher and a student, so I've never stopped investing my time in learning. Over the years, I've seen the powerful rewards manifested as lives saved, changed and mended. That's the true return on investment!

Chapter 26
Bobby Charlton – World Cup 1966

Winning Strategy:
Study the best.

One of my happiest memories is the 1966 World Cup games in England, which I had the privilege to see with Midge. It was our first time to England and on the same trip we also traveled to Scotland, Denmark, Norway, Germany, and France.

Bobby Charlton opened the scoring for England with a side-foot shot on goal in England vs. Portugal. During this game, the two goals by Charlton were very different. One was a technically proficient shot and the other was a power shot from 12 to 14 yards out. The power shot risked booing from the crowd for not being careful. Good power shots involve risk. To this day, people still debate it.

Sir Robert Charlton, as he is known today, was one of the best English midfielders of all time. He knew what to do under pressure, and whether to take the technical shot or the power shot was not a guess for him. He had probably already taken 5,000 or more power shots in his life.

English coaches think praise is weakness, so I wonder what Bobby heard from manager Alf Ramsey after he scored the two goals against Portugal. This win advanced England to the final where they won their only World Cup ever, against Germany, a game Midge and I also had the privilege to watch on July 30, 1966.

That was the last World Cup game televised in black and white. It was also the first World Cup broadcast live in England. At that time, ticket revenue was still very important. For the final, we stood (as did most spectators) in the end zone near a fan dressed in a top hat and a Union Jack. In 1966, the year England won the World Cup, footballers were working class heroes.

In 1966, Charlton was appearing in his third World Cup. His brother Jack was also on the World Cup team as a defender. Jack Charlton played for Leeds United and Bobby Charlton played for the legendary Manchester United Football Club in England, where he was celebrated for his long-range shots as well as his incredible endurance.

Unfortunately, a tragedy befell the Manchester United team in 1958 when a plane crash in Munich killed eight of the Manchester players and injured several others, including Bobby Charlton. In all 23 people died in the crash, including passengers and crew. Charlton was the first injured survivor to leave the hospital and travel back to England, setting the expectation for him to become a legend.

In the 1966 World Cup final against Germany, he and Franz Beckenbauer marked each other closely. Effectively, they marked each other out of the game, but England won 4-2 after extra time. Watching the World Cup game, I knew I was seeing the best of the best "footballers" of the era. To become the best at what I do, which is coaching, I study the best.

In 2008, Bobby Charlton's brother Jack presented him with the BBC Sports Personality Lifetime Achievement Award, for which he received a standing ovation. Though he came from a family of professional players (four uncles, a cousin, and his older brother), he gave credit to his mother and grandfather for his early development as a player. As a "footnote," this goes to show the importance of parent and grandparent coaches!

Chapter 27
Spring Arbor

Winning Strategy:
You always have more to give.

Ahead of the World Cup trip to Europe, it was my charge in 1966 to piece together all the hosting facets of Graduate Day as public relations director at Gordon College in Massachusetts.

The entire college gathered to hear the guest speaker, Dr. David McKenna, president of Spring Arbor College in Michigan. He shared a message about how vision can lead to significant change. The case in point was his vision to lead Spring Arbor Community College to become a four-year college. (It is now known as Spring Arbor University.)

About that time, after seven years at Gordon College, Taylor University in Upland, Indiana, invited me to serve as executive vice president. By that time, I had a clear vision that whatever I did or wherever I went, soccer had to be part of the package. Taylor University, however, was famous for football and basketball. Football at the school was coached by former UCLA All American Bob Davenport, and Don Odle's basketball teams were all but unbeaten.

While sitting in the gigantic living room of Taylor's president Milo Rediger, surrounded by the board of trustees, Mrs. Rediger announced there was an emergency call for me. She said I could take the call in the president's library. I entered the room to see the blinking light of the phone, sitting on the most amazing desk. I have yet to see another one that comes close. The desk maintained the shape of the trunk of a tree and was polished to perfection, suggesting nothing could mar or penetrate it. Sealed below the transparent surface was a small, brass plaque that read, "This desk was carved from the giant oak tree that stood on the very spot where this desk now sits."

On the other end of the call was Spring Arbor's president, Dr. McKenna.

"Whatever you do please do not sign anything!" he said.

"There's nothing to sign, since Taylor does not have a soccer program, nor will it will be establishing one in the near future," I replied.

I never asked, but I was quite sure I heard a sigh of relief on the other end.

Fast forward: I returned to Gordon and soon received a follow-up call from Dr. McKenna inviting me to visit Spring Arbor. The college happens to be situated in an unincorporated area, 75 miles west of Detroit and about a 40-minute drive from Michigan State University to the north. McKenna wanted me to come to Spring Arbor as director of public relations and to start a men's soccer program. However, after the Taylor meeting, I avowed to go anywhere with city noise and bus fumes, but not manure!

Nonetheless, within the week, Midge and I were on a plane to Michigan and on to the country air of Spring Arbor. For the next two days, almost everyone in the college interviewed us, topped off with a tea (no wine in those days for Free Methodists). A most memorable moment came when a woman chided Midge, "Girlie, your skirt is too short!"

This was one of our first clues that Spring Arbor would be a much more conservative environment, but two weeks later, after significant praying, and some sage tips from executive vice president Lon Randall, who would become my lifelong friend, we announced our resignation from Gordon. Two more weeks, and I was on my way to Spring Arbor for orientation.

Dr. McKenna met me at the airport, electing to drive me to Manure Central personally. That's when the problem began. Halfway to our destination he said, "I've changed my mind!"

POW!

All my Detroit instincts began to boil with an impulsive urge to split his face with a well-placed fist. Luckily, he followed that almost gleefully with, "I've decided that you should be our new dean of students. Putting you in the public relations office will rob our students of a certain genius I heard about time and time again when researching your years at Gordon."

Thus, we began our tenure at Spring Arbor in July of 1967, where I held the fulltime post of dean of students in addition to men's head soccer coach. At Spring Arbor, I was faced with the challenge of introducing the sport for a second time since, like Gordon, soccer was replacing football. Being the dean of students and soccer coach in my home state of Michigan was a pure delight. My little family was growing as well, and soon Midge and I welcomed our second child, our son Stephen born in 1967. This was a busy and wonderful time of life!

On the professional side, I learned massive lessons working in a school where female students once risked expulsion for wearing too-short skirts. (The bygone rule was that the bottom of the skirt must touch the top of two Webster Dictionaries stacked on top of each other.) As a believer in reformed theology, it was an intriguing journey in a fundamentalist environment where salvation could be lost based on daily behavior. My close friends frequently asked me how I could function with such an opposite belief system. My answer was, "I'll just keep one arm around them!"

As for the coaching experience, there isn't enough time in this century to do justice to the question. Perhaps the best way to sum it up is to say that the same principles and attitudes Dorcas instilled in me with reference to succeeding in life were in full force at Spring Arbor.

The school had just recently transitioned from a two-year community college to a full-fledged four-year liberal arts college. The problem was they continued to view themselves as a community college. At the pep rally, the night before the first-ever soccer game, in 1967, I told the entire community that the college was suffering from an inferiority complex. This was even though the athletes I was coaching were just as talented as those I worked with at my previous two colleges. I shocked the entire crowd when I claimed that within three years we would be in the nationals!

It was a prophesy fulfilled in 1969 when Spring Arbor, in eight overtime periods, led by Steve Friebel, upset the #1-ranked and undefeated Eastern Connecticut 1-0, earning a place in the national championship semi-finals. (Friebel is a crazy fellow-Detroiter and another lifetime friend, an innovator and former Vancouver, Washington principal.)

If I didn't know it already, my Spring Arbor team proved to me that we always have more to give!

By then, Dr. McKenna had accepted the post of president at Seattle Pacific College (where he served from 1968 to 1982). It wouldn't be long until there was another phone call in my future when he asked me to join his staff in Washington as dean of students and men's soccer coach.

Once again, Lon Randall, who accompanied McKenna to Seattle, was the swing voter who got us to Seattle. Midge and I accepted the opportunity. Without ever seeing the house on the hill near the college, discovered by Randall, we bought it for $30,000 with a $10,000 down payment. All that was left to do was pack our belongings into a moving truck, and off we went. Midge, Stacey and Stephen flew to Seattle and I drove.

Chapter 28
Mike Ryan

Winning Strategy:
Share a love for the game.

"Well, the only thing I know about college soccer in the Northwest," I said to the man in black, "is what my college coach told me as chair of the NCAA National Soccer Committee."

The man went on stamping out the boundaries of the field with his feet while I gleefully reported how the NCAA committee denied "some redheaded guy" from UW the chance for his team to compete in the national tournament. The committee eventually relented since there were no rules for who qualified to play in postseason games.

"And how did that end? The University of San Francisco beats UW 16-0!" I finished, satisfied.

Mihail "Mike" Ryan took off his cap and from the corner of my eye, I could see his hair was rather reddish. Had I been facing him directly while giving this report, accompanied by my own gleeful expressions, I might have anticipated the soon-to-be emotional explosion not unlike a volcanic eruption.

With what appeared to be smoke emanating from his mouth, ears and neck, he blasted, "Well let me tell you a 'ting' (Irish for thing) about that!"

He continued at full volume. "We (the 'we' that intuitively told me he was the coach) were informed in late afternoon before our scheduled game in a nearby Seattle neighborhood, that we were to play the University of San Francisco the next night in San Francisco. We played the Seattle game, rushed about to get airline tickets, and landed the next day four hours before kickoff," he said.

"The airline lost our luggage, complete with uniforms, shoes, balls, and all the required items necessary for a team to compete. The University of San Francisco helped provide some shoes and T-shirts, multicolored and patterned shorts, a few pairs of soccer shoes, but not enough to cover every player. Some of whom played the game in street shoes," he finished. "Clearly, we were no match for the powerhouse that had previously competed in national championships."

In the tool shack, in a wheelchair, was Eddie Craggs, the city's field maintenance supervisor, and a future inductee into the U.S. Soccer Hall of Fame. Eddie's son George Craggs was the first person Mihail met in 1962 when he was looking for a local soccer team he could join. George "Whitey" Craggs was one of the most notorious soccer referees ever to don a whistle. (Unlike all other denizens of Northwest soccer, I never called him "Whitey" choosing always to address him as George. I even stood up for him on occasion telling the masses that he did a "pretty good job refereeing on occasion.")

I was destined to be friends with the Irishman for years to come. It was really my unbelievable good fortune to meet Mike Ryan and Eddie Craggs on my first day in Seattle, since both were the bedrock of the local soccer community. (Ryan was the first president of the Washington Youth Soccer Association and the Washington Women's Soccer Association.)

The threads of our lives intertwined thereafter and we lived and breathed soccer for decades, emotionally moved by beautiful games the way others are by great music or works of art. The implicit particles of the game were in his blood stream. He was an immaculate teacher who understood the game like few others and shared a love for the game that made soccer in the Northwest what it is today.

After 42 years of friendship, at the end of his last soccer season, he died in November 2012, and I gave his eulogy. Since my old friend is no longer with us, parts of this story are as much his as mine. However, I'm sure he would have a "ting" or two to say about my version of events, now and then.

Chapter 29
The Falcons – early days

Winning Strategy:
Friendship is the big reward.

In the early days of coaching the Falcons, when I first came to Seattle Pacific, we measured victory by how few goals teams scored against us the second time we met. It was a ragtag team in the beginning and a losing season in 1970.

A "win" for the Falcons finally came with a 4-4 tie with the University of Puget Sound. We scored our first goal of the year in that game against UPS and we scored it in the first four minutes, then they scored four goals in a row. By half time, we were down 4-1.

We huddled in a room under the pool, pipes crackling, and I went into Vince Lombardi mode, pulling out every halftime slogan. "Gentlemen, we have seen the heights of joy and the depths of grief."

I never said, ever, "We're going to win this game." Never said, "We'll beat this team." However, I didn't have a tolerance for guys who liked to win but didn't hate losing. What I did say, was "We have a responsibility to go out and do what we've been practicing

There were six teams in the conference at that time. The Irishman's team included eight of eleven starters who worked at the foundries or on ships and were not even in school. There were no rosters in those days.

Having previously created the Northeast Collegiate Soccer Conference in New England, (NCSC), the year after my arrival in Seattle, I set to work to create a northwest conference. In the spring of 1971, I gathered together representatives from every school in the Northwest and at the end of the day, we established the Northwest Collegiate Soccer Conference (NCSC). I served as commissioner for the NCSC for the next 22 years while at the same time holding the office of secretary-editor of the NCAA Soccer Rules Committee for 40 years.

Whereas at Gordon, I had Paul Sideropoulos, the handsome Greek god from Greece who scored 108 goals in four years, there were no foreign stars at Seattle Pacific in the early years. We had to build the team from scratch. I probably only had one player that had ever seen a soccer ball.

I said, "It's going to be tough."

The players said, "We can do it coach."

Though my first year at Seattle Pacific was a losing season, by my second year, the team was winning, and this momentum never changed. One of my players from this era was Chuck Sides, who was on my 1971 team. Chuck went to work for Seattle Pacific in student affairs soon after graduating, and he saw that the school was facing a cultural crisis.

I tried to bring some levity to the situation. Perhaps the question of spices (and cursing, drinking, smoking and other bad habits) seemed silly to me. We follow our impulses until they ossify and then a jackhammer is needed to change them. Whatever the case may be, I continued to smoke the infrequent cigar, have the occasional drink and use rough language when the Spirit moved me. This didn't sit well with some of the school's leaders.

Over the next four decades, the Seattle Pacific men's soccer program continued to excel on a national level. My teams consistently won, bringing home five NCAA National Championships and a National Coach of the Year Award for me as their head coach. This brought widespread national attention, but not for the school's Christian education that was (understandably) the top concern of the administration.

It would not end well for me as head coach.

Yet, several of the players from those earliest years (nearly 50 years ago) became my close lifelong friends. The blessing of the early Falcon glory days, the major enduring reward, is friendship. More than half of my dearest friends today are from the dawn of my time in Seattle. Those friendships are the real rewards and justification for attempting to do anything great. The golden trophies are the friendships found, the relationships grown, and the opportunities realized.

Chapter 30
The F Bomb

Winning Strategy:
Understand there will be tough times.

The year Joey Welker, my player from Gordon College, died in Vietnam, an American named Paul Cohen was arrested for wearing a jacket with the slogan "Fuck the Draft" emblazoned on it. His conviction was overturned by the U.S. Supreme Court, which decided that the public display of the f word is protected under the First and Fourteenth Amendments to the U.S. Constitution.

As an edifier, it's my mission to build people up. Edification is one of the reasons we are given spiritual gifts. In Greek, the word for education is *oikodone*, which translates literally as the building of a house. In the New Testament, Paul's letters use this word, translated as both education and edification in the context of spiritual progress by patient labor. We lovingly check each other's spiritual progress. MacVittie (a.k.a. "Pascal" and I have pledged such to each other for life.)

Whether to curse or not as a coach is not something I can preach about, but I can talk about the rules of engagement when one is part of a certain subculture. At a Christian school, there may be rules the group has adopted and believes to be important. This set of rules may include not dancing, not cursing, not playing cards, or not using salt and pepper, as it did at Seattle Pacific. Someone new to the group may not understand the origin or reasoning for some of the rules and may find it difficult to conform.

Although it is becoming increasingly common in society (films, politics, sports and business) to hear strong language, it still carries the expected shock value and ability to express emotion.

(Nonetheless, when it comes to cursing, I must mention my longstanding stance on never taking the Lord's name in vain, which is the biblical definition for profanity.)

Now, would Coach B, my Wheaton soccer coach, have cursed players, refs, or others? No, absolutely not.

Have I? Yes.

At the end of World War II, I stood with a crowd when they were burning effigies of Mussolini, Tito and Hitler. A child at the time, I thought they were burning real people. This was in a vacant lot in Detroit. As an 18 year old in 1954, I went down to enlist, but because of the loss of my two fingers and thumb, I was "4F" and they would not take me.

On November 22, 1963, when President Kennedy died, my right foot was just stepping off the field at Brookwood School in Massachusetts when George the custodian told me the news. I sobbed all weekend with the rest of the country.

When Kent State students were shot by the National Guard while protesting in May of 1970, I was at Spring Arbor College, not too far away. By then I was in the suspicious category of people over 30.

The signs of the times said, "We Don't Agree."

PART III

Chapter 31
Creating a Winning Team

Winning Strategy:
Provide the framework, then let go.

I enjoy winning, some may say, at all costs. It's not part of my nature simply

to praise the effort, as is common nowadays, with participation awards for

everyone. That may be appropriate for small children, but there comes a time

when outcomes matter.

So how does a coach create a winning team? The *Harvard Business*

Review interviewed Bill Walsh, the Stanford football coach who went on to

coach the San Francisco 49ers to three Super Bowl wins. One thing he did

differently than other coaches was focus on the "minutiae" of practices,

orchestrating every minute.

That's something I recall about Coach B.'s winning strategy at

Wheaton. Precise practices with no down time are part of the winning formula I learned early on. It is very important for players to be receptive to coaching on the field, and this begins with practice. I don't want to waste precious time overruling because it takes time and patience to develop a strong team.

First, I create a framework to allow failure, which is an important part of the learning and growing process. Early losses for the team may really be big wins in the end. Failure in the beginning is desirable.

Next, enthusiasm matters. Personal coaching styles will vary at this point. At Seattle Pacific University, there were times when the failure to maximize my team's performance led to scorching, half-time speeches (so-called pep talks) aimed at the team, and sometimes, individual players. Most of such deliveries created positive results. However, I also served as dean of students for the college, so perhaps I learned to be more reserved in dealing with negative situations, on and off the field. Only a fool speaks without thinking.

Believe me, absolutely no one wants to hear the coach whining and complaining about how unfair it all is. Coaching is an opportunity for personal growth and spiritual unfolding, and the sooner the better. Why we do what we do, once the onion is peeled, is the beat underneath. There is an inner voice urging me to come up to a higher level of expression. Call that the Holy Spirit, God, or Instinct.

Back to brass tacks, the third key element to training the team is building endurance, strength and speed, which are hallmarks of great athletes. I include these in every practice session, no matter how elite the players may be. These attributes of sustained performance are required to ensure success.

Repeating something often enough, moves the athlete closer to perfection, with a sixth sense for anticipation. This works beyond sports in that if it is true that an athlete improves anticipation through training, an executive may do the same. Anticipating next moves leads to peak performance.

A good coach (or parent, or boss) builds a strong foundation to give the team roots and wings. More recently, there is a trend to intense specialized sports training in youth athletes. Not only does this increase injuries, it isn't good for building a strong team.

One of my favorite examples is John McKay, the University of Southern California coach whose teams won four national championships and went to nine Rose Bowl games. In 2014, he was named the All-Century Coach of the Rose Bowl during the celebration of the 100th Rose Bowl game.

McKay was popular in the press for witty one-liners, so people may have missed the coaching lessons he had to offer from his decades of experience. In an interview with *The New York Times*, after his retirement from coaching professional football (he headed to the NFL after USC), he emphasized that player specialization was out of hand.

Coaching players to be utility players is an interesting proposition. In soccer, the "Dutch Swirl" is a cerebral concept created by Dutch coaches in the 1970s. In this theory, every player should be a utility player, able to play any position at any time. A utility player is one who plays several positions well. This is a term used more often in baseball, but it applies to many sports, from football to water polo to soccer. Versatility is an asset to any team.

One of my utility players who rode the "pine patrol" for the Falcons was Darren, a reserve player and back-up goalie for four years at SPU. During this time, we won two national championships in 1985 and 1986. I ran into Darren recently at a birthday wine tasting event near Seattle. He is now a high-level business executive running one of the largest printing companies in the country. He said the legacy I created of striving for excellence as a team carried over into the careers of his teammates, including several extremely successful business leaders.

This attitude filtered all the way down to tryouts. There was an expectation of never giving up that began with the first practice and extended to the championship games, even though often we were not the most talented team on the field. Beginning with a mandate to fail, any team can be a winning team with the right coaching, capitalizing on group strengths.

Chapter 32
Critical Assumptions

Winning Strategy:
Discover your strengths and weaknesses.

The Harvard forum in Cambridge, Massachusetts, brought in world figures

to speak, and as a coach for nearby Gordon College, I received an invitation

to attend. On one occasion, the president of Harvard wrote an essay on the

subject of "Critical Assumptions." Although it was 50 years ago, this made a

lasting impact on me and became one of the most valuable and versatile of all

winning strategies.

Critical assumptions fill the spaces between information gathered to

make an important decision. When a decision must be made without 100

percent of the facts, or with imperfect knowledge (nearly always), critical

assumptions are required. In the years since I first heard this concept

introduced by Harvard University's 24th president, Dr. Nathan Pusey, it has become an important business theory. (Critical assumptions are called "CAs" in business-world shorthand.)

A gap in information is often the case for a coach before the season begins and the skill and spirit of the players under game pressure is not yet tested. Yet some decisions are time-sensitive and require action without all the facts. An example of this would be who to keep on the team and who to cut after tryouts. This requires critical assumptions to bridge the unknown.

In other areas of life, very important personal decisions such as marriage require critical assumptions as well. Prior to marriage, many facts are unknown, and will only become a reality later during the marriage. Without all the knowledge and wisdom that will come with time, critical assumptions are essential.

Critical thinking (rational rather than emotional) is necessary for anticipating the future, and we all do it as part of our earthly existence. Assumptions have earned a very bad reputation, and this is because most people don't bake risk into the pie. Some critical assumptions will fail. That is the risk taken into consideration when it isn't possible for all facts to be known.

In business, critical assumptions are ideas that must prove true in the real world for the venture to be successful. Assumptions based on emotions go awry and lead to poor outcomes. Critical assumptions (CAs) combine critical thinking with the need to anticipate the future as well as possible. Once all information available is gathered and critical assumptions bridge the gaps, it becomes possible to evaluate the level of risk and potential impact of a new strategy.

In the 1978 national championships that Seattle Pacific won against Alabama A&M, we might have been seen as brilliant had we just conceded the game to the massively talented internationally populated team of gazelles, and headed back to Seattle. Instead, our collective attitude to the man was that since we earned our way to the final, we would play with ferocity.

Knowing my team was out-skilled, I made the critical assumption that this would lead to more scoring opportunities for Alabama in our defensive zone. Thus, I decided to use five defensive backs in an era when typically only two took this positioning. We set about to take what knowledge we had and maximize it to win. And we did win, 1-0, in three overtimes!

Even when a team's experience or expertise is less than perfect, understanding how to use critical assumptions is a way to build strong bridges over weaknesses that help the team succeed.

Chapter 33
Defense

Winning Strategy:
Man has a right to choose his attitude.

I expect most people have heard the phrase, "Keep your friends close and your enemies closer!" It was made famous by the character Michael Corleone in *The Godfather Part II* (1974). It is a variation of Sun-Tzu, an ancient Chinese military strategist who said, "Know your enemy and know yourself and you will always be victorious."

When I first heard this utterance "light years" ago, it seemed contrary to everything I had learned about opponents and enemies in early life. In fact, anyone in the role of the opposition was not only the enemy, I once thought he or she was to be hated, despised and eliminated.

Once my Christian verities kicked in, it changed my intellectual view of the notion, but not my emotional approach to the issue. While studying at

Gordon in the 1960s, my thinking began to change when I discovered Viktor Frankl's book *Man's Search for Meaning*, which bears witness to the fact that regardless the issue "...man has the right to choose his attitude."

If that statement were made by Warren Buffet or Bill Gates today, the general reaction would most likely bring with it not a little scorn of the ilk, "Oh, yeah, easy for them to say, blah blah blah!" However, the background for Frankl's statement was Auschwitz concentration camp, the largest of the Nazi death camps, where he was a prisoner during World War II. His mother, brother and wife died at the camp, where life expectancy was less than two weeks. Yet he lasted more than two and a half years. After liberation, he returned to the University of Vienna to join his former colleagues, who begged him to write a scathing indictment against the German people. He refused.

Instead, he wrote *Man's Search for Meaning*, based on his life research. The book came out in 1946 in Vienna, and in 1959 in the U.S. It sold millions of copies worldwide and was named one of the 10 most influential books of the 20th Century. In his book, Frankl describes his own personal experiences as a concentration camp prisoner. The compelling premise from Frankl is:

Everything can be taken from a man but one thing: the last of the human freedoms to choose one's attitude in any given set of circumstances.

He believed the four things that led to survival were a sense of purpose, a spiritual belief in God, a rich inner or intellectual life and communicating and receiving thoughts from loved ones. He called this theory logotherapy. The principles to take away are that life has meaning even in the most miserable of circumstances, that our motivation for living is to find meaning in life, and we have freedom to find meaning in what we do and experience.

Applying this theory, what is to be gained by complaining? Who is watching and listening to me as a coach? What will the reaction gain? What are the long-term impacts? I have the power to choose my attitude and behavior in every situation. Call it the golden rule of defense: Choose attitude with care.

In soccer, of course, there are tangible physical elements to success, but mental attitude is every bit as important. All players in all positions must be taught how to defend, physically and with mental preparedness. As a metaphor and lesson for life, coaching players to understand that one's attitude in any situation is a matter of choice, is indispensible to the growth of the player, as well as to the lifelong well-being of the individual.

Chapter 34
God's Purpose

Winning Strategy:
There is a time for everything.

I never forget to employ a formula to establish the expectation of superior performance in the minds of my players. When we begin our initial meetings both individually and as a team, I open with, "If you think this is just about soccer, go home now!"

I close sessions with, "Whether you believe in God or not, this team exists for the glory of God and it is our purpose to honor Him in all we do."

For example, if we win, may we do so with grace and kindness. If we do not win, may we be noble in defeat. In day-to-day actions, there are things that remind my players of our mandate.

What is God's purpose and how do we find it? As a college student, I thought I wanted to be an attorney. Instead, I found myself on a completely different path guiding students and players through their early years of adulthood. I enjoyed argument and persuasion, but nowadays, I say, "I'm not in the saving business, but I know someone who is."

The road I am traveling involves protecting, defending and looking after people in many ways. This became clear in the wee hours of the early morning years ago in Boston. It was after the arrival of Dr. Bill Wordon as dean of students at Gordon College in the 1960s. At the time, he was working on *Personal Death Awareness,* a book based on his research interviews with suicide-attempt survivors and others. He went on to lecture at Harvard Medical School and authored many books on grief counseling.

During my time at Gordon, over a six-year period, I took every course available in seminary except Hebrew. I was doing it for my own edification rather than to be a minister, or so I thought. On one night, however, a call came to our little apartment at 3 a.m., and God's purpose was for me to be prepared for that moment.

My wife Midge was next to me as I spoke to a young student on the verge of suicide, threatening to jump from the bridge of an overpass into traffic. From somewhere within me, I knew the first thing to do was neutralize her thinking. Arguing, "Don't jump," doesn't work. Instead, I acknowledged that, "Whatever compelled you at 3 a.m. to jump from the overpass, it must be really bad or upsetting. Things must be pretty bad. It's got to be, I understand, but why now?"

Whatever she answered would be the bridge to lead her out of it.

"Things are so terrible," she said.

Any answer would be the hook to pull her back. By the time we finished talking, she promised me she would not jump. Many years later, about 30 years after moving to Seattle, there was an unexpected thank you letter. She was married to a lawyer, she said, and they had three great kids.

God has given us gifts and strengths and these are not limited. There may be as many gifts as there are needs. Gifts of wisdom, discernment, words, healing, hospitality, mercy, giving and serving are mentioned throughout the Bible as well as gifts of craftsmanship, composing music, prose and poetry, teaching, leadership and governing. One thing that helps in discovering God's purpose is being receptive to the needs of people. God helps us find purpose through other people. Coaching is a blessing if for this reason alone!

"To everything there is a season, and a time to every purpose under the heaven."

(Ecclesiastes 3:1)

Chapter 35
Accountability in Action

Winning Strategy:
Shut down, don't knock down.

On a soccer team, the goalkeeper is responsible for defending the goal and the defenders are responsible for making the goalkeeper's job as easy as possible by minimizing the shots on goal. Often when my team gave up a goal, it was due to the other team executing a great play. If everyone did their jobs and was in position and the other team scored on a great play, so be it. They earned it. No one was to blame. But sometimes, we gave up a goal due to a defender or the goalkeeper making an error and a common error was playing out of position.

Maybe the other team scored an easy goal because one of my defenders got out of position making an offensive run toward the other goal when he knew he was responsible for staying in his own end. Perhaps a goalkeeper wandered far outside the box to provide offensive support and could not get back in time to defend a breakaway. When my players made errors, they knew it. I knew it. I held them accountable. No excuses.

During a game, all of my players knew their responsibilities. All were responsible to field their positions. Some may have had a responsibility to mark a specific member of the opposing team. And each player on the field understood, barring injury, he was responsible to stay in the game until I either substituted for him or the game ended. That meant not getting a red card, which would automatically remove him from the game and leave the team shorthanded.

When I was a player, I would try to right a wrong by virtue of being the faster and tougher player. I did not go for playing dirty, and I train my teams the same way with this little speech:

"Shut down, don't knock down. If you knock down, then maybe you'll feel better for a moment, but you wind up paying dearly for it because original sin is never punished in soccer. It is always the retaliation that is seen. Some players will spit on you when the referee is looking the other way. Spit washes off. But if you cold-cock a player after he spits on you, you've just allowed him to win. He got you good. Moreover, you're the one who will get the red card, which will hurt your team tremendously. "

It happened to one of my players named Ricky. He was the fastest person on the team and a sweeper who I converted from a forward. We played the University of Ireland in a tournament and all of sudden, he's out of the game with a red card.

"What happened?" I asked.

And he said, "Well, I cold-cocked him."

I said, "Of course you did. I saw it. We all saw it."

He said, "Well, he spit on me."

I shook my head and said, "He spit on you? Well, they spit on Jesus, too. And they hit him with rocks and thorns and everything else and he didn't say a word." I said, "That doesn't mean you're Jesus, but it does mean you are smart enough not to retaliate."

Ricky was one of the brightest players I ever had, earning straight A's even though athletics caused him to miss class frequently. He went on to make millions in the stock market.

He struggled with the pride factor that day, but Ricky was a man who held himself accountable for his actions. Dorcas would have liked him. I know I did. And still do!

Chapter 36
The Power of Attitude

Winning Strategy:
Hard work beats talent when talent doesn't work hard.

One of the early warnings I issued to my teams (and now to corporate groups) is: "Hard work beats talent when talent doesn't work hard!"

There are substantial examples in history – including my personal history – that validate this principle. Coaching transcends sport. A parent who gets a kid to go to bed without World War III breaking out is a successful coach. A manager who motivates people to achieve company goals is a successful coach.

Some people have genius or talent or both. One definition of genius is found in the 18th Century French *Encycolopedie*. "He whose soul is more expansive and struck by the feelings of all others; interested by all that is in nature never to receive an idea unless it evokes a feeling; everything excites him and on which nothing is lost."

It seems that an element of genius, then, is in fact, one's attitude of interest in all people and things. All that is necessary for greatness is a winning attitude backed by hard work, and an interest in life itself, which leads to a desire to improve constantly in all areas.

At the same time, it is a given, proven repeatedly by my teams, that regimental training (game fitness and readiness) does not guarantee success (defined as winning). However, it will certainly give an edge over less properly prepared individuals and teams.

In the 1978 national championship game, Seattle Pacific faced a far superior team in the areas of skill and innate soccer knowledge, but not necessarily stamina. To a man, the Alabama A&M players were far more refined with reference to their soccer skills and clearly more superior physically, particularly when it came to speed and quickness. Many of the players were recruited from Nigeria, where soccer is the most popular national sport.

Even more daunting, Seattle Pacific lost the national championship game to this same team the year before, in 1977, so we knew exactly what to expect in terms of their talent and skill. In effect, this was the Nigerian national team masquerading as Alabama A&M University, and the players on the other team had the advantage of a lifetime of practiced muscle reaction time. The result is superior anticipation.

Yet they did not win. Regular game time ended with a draw at 0-0, and we then entered one, two and then three overtime periods, playing to the point that the A&M team's endurance flagged. Though very talented, they had grown accustomed to defeating inferior teams with ease. On the other hand, the attitude of the Falcons was that we would do everything in our power to win, giving it our all.

The result was that in 1978, Seattle Pacific took Alabama A&M, 1-0 in triple overtime to win the national championship! This was our fourth national championship final in five years, and in each of the previous attempts, we ended as runner-up.

One of the most vivid images I recall from that game in the Miami heat was the two teams on the outside of the field next to a small lake during the halftime break. The Alabama team spread out along the opposite side of the lake, most propped up against the trunks of trees, looking exhausted, with white salt marks running down the sides of their long-sleeved, purple soccer jerseys. Our guys, shirtless – and hydrated up to their ears - were collectively peeing in the pond.

When the final – and only goal of the game was scored in the third overtime, at 1:26:47 of the game, the Falcons were leaping and shouting, hugging and dancing while the Alabama players were spread across the field like dead fish washed up on a beach.

Our first NCAA National Champion title in 1978 was a sweet victory! Shortly after the win, the NCAA presented me with the honors of NCAA Division II National Coach of the Year.

Chapter 37
Creativity and Vision

Winning Strategy:
Guide your players to become good decision makers.

The concept of creativity and vision in fast-paced environments, such as soccer, requires strong and quick decision making by the players on the field. A coach can't rely entirely on a player to fill in the creative piece without training in this area. Creativity separates the elite players from the non-elite players and excellent coaches from the rest.

An environment of creativity hones vision during training practices. Starting with a mandate to fail, players are at first allowed to make good and bad decisions. Finally, when asked what they could have done better, the critical thinking begins flowing. Later, they will know what happens as a result of various decisions, good and bad. In this way, an excellent coach guides players in practice to become good decision makers come game day.

For instance, in the 1985 NCAA Division II championships, we (the Falcons) had a 3-0 lead going into the second half of the final against Florida International University. Then the other team scored two goals. How to protect a lead is a crucial decision. This type of judgment should be a matter of routine learned through drills. Rehearsing lead-protection in practice makes it easy to understand and later execute. During the 1985 championships, for example, my players Peter Hattrup and Scott Cairns paced the game, and we shut FIU down, winning 3-2.

With the U.S. Women's team in Taiwan, the strategy to protect the lead was something I explained ahead of the World University Games. The team chose the name "Nubber" for the play, and used it in every game. The concept is to shrink the field to the flanks of the opponent's penalty area, kick the ball to the corner and continue in one quadrant for tighter ball control. The elite group of All-American women athletes executed the play to perfection, winning again, and again.

Keeping the game isolated by holding play to one small area is a way to let the clock become the 12th man on the field, protecting the lead. Playing the controlled game requires vision and discipline because it is crucial not to foul.

Other situations will require even more creativity and vision, combined with good decisions by players on the field. In the 1993 NCAA semifinal, we played against a Florida team that could have been called "Leigh-on-Sea" because there were nine (pro?) English players on the roster. The team was winning easily and by an average of five goals or better over the other teams.

How we won the semifinal game against this team is all about creativity because as far as technical skills go, we were not the better team. Amazingly, we were ahead 3-2 with less than a few seconds to go when they tied the score. Nine minutes into the final OT, we were trailing 3-5 and managed to score twice in 61 seconds to force penalty kicks which we won – at 12:40 a.m. (well past midnight) 10-9!

A word about endurance is again necessary. Coaches can, should/must include in daily training sessions elements of endurance, strength and speed training. Endurance comes from creating greater oxygen-carrying capacity. Strength comes from weight training, which was unheard of in basketball, soccer, ice hockey and several other sports as recently as 20 to 30 years ago. Speed training comes from sprint exercises as well as asymmetrical running, but it doesn't end there. Psychological/mental preparation is critical, too.

The point is that success in competition is the consequence of proper physical training, but there is also a reservoir of possibilities in psychological and mental preparation.

We won the 1993 semifinal game due to mental strength, guts and stamina. Two nights later, in a game as boring as watching grapes turn to raisins, the Falcons won the NCAA Division II National Championship in a 1-0 game against Southern Connecticut State.

Chapter 38
Power Shots

Winning Strategy:
Focus on what you can control.

When the kid from the bench comes to my side and says, "I'll try, coach!" I say, "Go back and sit on the bench!"

"I'll try is an excuse – a buffer – for those who fear failure! I want players who say, "I'LL DO IT, Coach!"

In short, dare to fail. (See Thomas Edison and the Wright Brothers.)

When coaching a team, focus on what is controllable as a coach. This could be teaching technical skills, bringing tactical awareness, or fine-tuning psychological factors.

Tactical awareness means knowing where and when and why to move the ball at the proper time. Technical skills such as ball control, passing, heading, and tackling are basic requirements, and though there needs to be an emphasis on speed and direction, attitude is indispensable. The fact is, every shot on goal will not score, but the player must believe that every shot will score -- that is essential!

A coach can control the psychological factors of attitude and effort to a certain degree. When it comes to taking shots on goal, this is fundamental because without successful shots on goal, there are no wins.

A finesse shot, which is a technically proficient shot, is different from a power shot, and perhaps the best way to explain the difference is that a finesse shot is more like a pass, using the inside of the foot to place the ball to one side or the other of the goalie. (One of my threadbare shouts during shooting drills is, "The goalkeeper is not a target; he/she is an obstacle to be missed!") A power shot, on the other hand, is a hard driven ball. Knowing when to do what kind of shot improves with time on the ball. The player's confidence while shooting is also something the coach can control by practicing shots on goal in a tight area with small-sided teams.

The other difference between a power shot and a finesse shot is that the power shot is done with the top part of the foot (bootlaces). Although it is very powerful, it is less accurate than other types of shots. Yet, there are times when a power shot is more appropriate than a finesse shot. Again, most important to the power shot is confidence. The player must completely believe he will make the shot and have no doubt because with the head down, he/she may not even see the goal.

There are plenty of technique explanations about the power shot, such as pointing the toe down and planting the non-shooting foot toward the goal. Usually, for this type of shot, power is generated from high up the leg in the thigh, rather than the calf. More crucial than technique, a lack of confidence means a lack of power and missed opportunities.

What can be controlled begins with attitude. Attitude is much more under the control of the coach than player talent. Talent is nice to have, but attitude wins championships. The attitude the coach wants to cultivate is one of being coachable, hardworking, and high energy. Commitment to the team is also vitally important.

Chapter 39
Coaching Your Own Kids

Winning Strategy:
Celebrate time with your children.

What is it like to have children? Quick answer: AWESOME. Mesmerizingly wonderful. My children's births were the eighth and ninth wonders of the world. Same with my grandchildren...one, of whom, I was in the birth room to see born. The journey, with detours and some of the usual calamities of life (illnesses, broken this and that...) has been phenomenal and is still going!

My daughter Stacey was born in Beverly Hospital in Beverly, Massachusetts. Midge and I were living in a small, one-room apartment in the basement of Conrad Hall, a brand new three-story, 13-room dormitory for Gordon College, one of four such buildings. We lived off Route #128, which runs from Cape Ann on the north shore to the more famous Cape Cod on the south shore in sight of Nantucket's Hyannis Port Kennedy Compound.

But back in our tiny dwelling where, to give the illusion of more space we slept on a hide-a-bed, at oh dark hundred the morning of Friday the 13th of December, Midge said, "I think we better go to the hospital!"

Still, in an early morning stupor, I replied (the still reiterated comment every anniversary since --that's 55 years folks), "Are you sure it's not just a feeling of discomfiture?"

All incredulity aside, off we went to Beverly Hospital where I, unceremoniously dropped mother-to-be before heading to Manchester, where I taught at the Brookwood (pre-prep) School as THE science teacher for grades first through eighth. First graders learned how to boil water; eighth graders learned how to forecast weather with balloons sent miles into the atmosphere.

As the noon hour neared, the school secretary stuck her nose into the class and said, "Mr. McCrath, you're wanted at the hospital!"

Just as I was leaving the school, the secretary asked, "What do you want, a boy or a girl?"

I said, "If it's a girl, it will take an Act of Congress to get her in my house!"

In no time at all I raced the little green VW Beatle from Manchester to the next village of Beverly. Upon entering the maternity floor, the nurse immediately announced that I was the father of a healthy, seven-pound ...G-I-R-L!!!!! (Deep breaths!) (Shock!) (Whaaaat?)

However, as I pressed my face against the glass of the nursery to see my daughter, I knew there would be no need for congressional action. Our little baby girl showed a tiny hint of grayish, blond fuzz on a nearly bald head. Not to worry, proud Daddy strutted into Mom's room to finalize what to name this child!

Back to Brookwood School, although not physically because I remained at the hospital for another couple of hours. Etched in my mind were the names of Steve and Stacey Pendleton, two of the most beautiful, well-behaved, intelligent children I ever encountered. I mean beeeauuutiiifullll human beings! The only thing remaining was what middle name to choose? An earlier muse for a middle name for Stacey was Michelle or Lynette - something like that. The compromise was a customized Lynelle which, sadly, but not surprisingly, has never sat well with Stacey.

Stephen, aka Steve aka Seve was born on Halloween 1967 in Jackson (Michigan) Memorial Hospital. The archaic law forbidding husband to be in the birthing room was still in effect. However, this time there was no resistance from Dad and no mention of "discomfiture." But, like his sister before him the call came in the wee hours of the morning. Unlike his sister, his arrival came shortly after arrival at the hospital.

Also, unlike the drop and flee "Dad" was guilty of on December 13, 1963, I headed for the grossly overheated waiting room, plopped into an oversized leather chair, and promptly fell asleep. Sometime later, I was shocked awake by a female voice shouting, "Coach McCrath, YOU HAVE A SON!"

Startled and in a half-conscious state, I jumped to my feet, hopped two or three times in no particular direction, then stared at my son cradled in the nurse's left arm for what seemed an inordinately long time. I then spoke, and said, "He looks like Winston Churchill!" As aforementioned, his first name was predestined leaving only a second name, which wasn't a problem. My first name is Charles and has been a family name in the MacRae (McCrath) clan for more than 500 years.

Seve and Stacey came with me to Northwest Soccer Camp from their earliest memory. That was in the early 1970s. When they grew up, sports continued to be a big part of their lives. It's hard to believe they are both in their 50s now. Where did the time go? As a parent and a grandparent, my goal is to create the proper support where my kids and grandkids can learn truth, discipline, love and freedom within a framework of restraint. Boundaries provide the opportunities to define one's freedom.

I never had a family from which to glean normal family values even though most of the early years were spent in the care of a godly mother. Although she was plagued by heart and other medical problems, she weathered all the storms and hazards of a single parent. My brother and I were two highly spirited boys and I was a human missile carrying a payload of devilish destruction with every step I took. Yet she prevailed and managed to bequeath values (many detours notwithstanding) to both sons.

My daughter's oldest is Keith Charles Smith, born January 5, 1998. Her youngest is Stephen Reilly Smith, born March 20, 2001, which was the first day of spring, and it snowed in Seattle that day! My son Steve and his wife Katie's two children are Kieran Charles Micah McCrath, born March 11, 2015, and Sienna Ashleigh Ruth McCrath, born January 5, 2017. Thus, my oldest and youngest grandchildren were born on the same day, the 5th of January.

My own children might describe me as at once crazy, loving, caring, creative, generous, gregarious, funny/hilarious, talented, diverse, loyal to them and their mother (and her second husband), intelligent, if not brilliant, minimally famous and there for them! I'm also very proud of them. In the early years, I was absent too much of the time!

Many coaches are too hard on their own kids and expect more from them than other players, which strains relationships leading to regrets later. From my vantage point now, it's important to celebrate the all-too-short time with one's kids and grandchildren. Grandparents and grandparent-coaches get second chances to help define love.

Chapter 40
Player Conduct

Winning Strategy:
Always leave a place better than you find it.

How should players conduct themselves on and off the field? I will double back now to my opening statements to every team I coached, "If you think this is just about soccer, go home now."

In my opinion, this statement was – and continues to be – the bedrock of every principle I felt compelled to pass on to my players and colleagues alike. In this vein was a phrase I introduced to the entire team and repeated when we checked into hotels or dined in restaurants on the road, "Always leave a place better than you find it."

I brought the phrase to life with examples such as not leaving a hotel room looking like a drunken brawl occurred. I painted pictures for my young players to improve their capacity for empathy, amplifying that the maid is not one's servant. Although they may never see the housekeeping staff, I said, they should be aware that the person cleaning the rooms is simply not a slave. Perhaps she is a single mother, working hard to take care of her family, and has few employment options for various reasons.

"When you finish with your towels," I explained clearly, "drape them over the tub and place your waste materials in the containers provided as opposed to scattered around the room. The washcloths ARE NOT shoe shine rags. You are free to take the shampoo with you but DO NOT STEAL objects, clothes hangers, paintings, remote controls, towels, etc. from the room. Be kind to waitresses, bus drivers, maintenance workers and people in general when you are out and about. DO NOT SLUR OR SLANDER opponents, fans, referees or make inappropriate comments to women. When nightfall comes do not bring a 'date' into the hotels." (These are strong words, but young men sometimes need to hear them.)

As to whether this concept for noble behavior and character is valid today, the subject is just as important as ever. Some may think the X, Y, and Z generations have had the world handed to them on a silver platter and that kids are somehow less sensitive to the needs of others. This is likely untrue. I expect the best from my players today in the same way that I did 30, 40 and 50 years ago. Courteous behavior is an important part of character and it will always be something I expect and challenge all of my players to uphold.

Chapter 41
Chess

Winning Strategy:
Beauty on the field.

There is no divine right to score.

The Dutch play an intensely cerebral form of soccer called "Total Football" that came from coach Rinus Michels, who FIFA named Coach of the Century in 1999. The foundation of this Dutch coaching style is making every player a utility player, one who can play any position. No player has a fixed role. This strategy came about in the 1970s when the Dutch teams were very powerful.

Pro players since the '70s often think of soccer like chess, and there are some strong parallels between chess and soccer. Chess helps a player anticipate next moves by reading and analyzing the game.

A finite passing game, simple and controlled, is characteristic of the Total Football style. Most soccer games stay in the middle third of the field.

This type of game is also called the Dutch swirl, (like an orange swirl, because the Dutch national team wears orange and white).

With this type of control, today's players, if they have a two-goal lead with three minutes left, should never lose. It is possible to make a coaching career out of high-pressure offense in the opponent's back third. Shrink the field, play in one little quadrant, and again, the players must have discipline and not foul.

Another drill I created to prepare my team before a national championship game in Florida is known, perhaps throughout the world, as the BAHIA. Before describing it, there must be a story - always a story when it comes to Cliffy Boy. It was 1986 and we began the season on a huge downer, which settled into our collective hive mind following an interruption to preseason training. In the middle of "two-a-days" at SPU's Camp Casey on Whidbey Island, the site of our annual training camp, the news came as a shock.

Pre-season training began as usual that year and the formula for selecting our team was to begin with a camp roster of any-and-all prospects who desired to try-out for the team. Some years there were more than 70 preseason players, making it a daunting task to trim the number to 24. Once in camp, we were required to fax (pre-email) the roster to the university registrar, who, in turn, would return a fax listing the academically eligible players. This process took a few days. Only those players enrolled at the university and in good academic standing could continue at camp.

The unexpected news from the registrar that year was a total SHOCKER! Midway through the week, we were informed that our superstar player and leading scorer Peter was no longer eligible. Further research revealed that he wasn't even registered and did not attend class in the spring quarter. I hasten to say that Peter, the son of an accomplished lawyer and world-famous sailing mother, is one of THE most intelligent and critical thinkers on the planet.

Peter eventually went on to a very successful pro-soccer career that spanned 17 years, which demonstrates just how good he was. In his previous three years at Seattle Pacific, he scored 65 goals and was an easy pick to break the 68-goal scoring record of Bruce Raney. Without a doubt, as players and coaches, we were unhappy about the news. That notwithstanding, I reiterated (preached?) my longstanding philosophy that no team should expect to win with a star system lest opponents shutdown the star and render that team impotent. So, out of the starting gates we came with a fury.

Our opening three games were played in Chico, California, in the Far West Classic, an annual, eight-team early season competition I had created years before. We scored a total of 11 goals, allowed the competition zero and headed off to Florida with a new name for the team: The Smurfs. I'm not exactly sure why, because the cartoon Smurfs are blue, whereas Seattle Pacific Falcon colors are maroon and white. The Smurfs were a popular animated series in the 1980s, and the little blue characters lived in a community sharing a kind environment and adventures that emphasized the contribution of all members. Papa Smurf is the leader of the Smurf community, so perhaps that was me!

Basically, it was a team full of no-names who could smash any opponent, although that was about to change, abruptly. The next two games in Miami, not only ended in defeat, we scored no goals against our opponents, teams we would have handled easily with Peter in the lineup. Depression set in. Heavily. What happened over the next 47 hours not only transformed the team, it altered my approach to coaching forever.

I felt a team meeting was needed to restore our early season success or at least give the guys a chance to talk it out. If nothing else, it might let the team know I cared. On our trip to Florida, we stayed in the luxurious Bahia Mar Hotel, mere yards from the Atlantic Ocean. (I sometimes think our coast-to-coast travel schedule had more to do with attracting star recruits than our school's academic offerings or the obvious good looks and brilliance of the coach!)

It was not my custom to pay for meeting rooms, particularly since I had talked the Bahia Mar into giving us the $125 rooms for $18 each. When making travel plans two months earlier, the wonderful Louisa roared when I said $18 after she quoted me the $125 for the Bahia Mar. However, knowing tourist season was over, I convinced her by saying we would take 18 rooms for two weeks and would only need an occasional change of towels. In any event, I managed to find a dimly lit ballroom for the team meeting, and told them to straggle in one by one so as not to call attention to our unauthorized use of the room.

The Falcon players sat theater style down near the front of the stage where I hiked up and began addressing the team. My message was simple. We all knew Peter was gone and agreed to the notion that we all had to buck up and play as a team. This we did in the first three games, but chickened out against tougher competition in Florida.

The first game in Miami was against Florida International University, a team we defeated in the 1985 national championship in Seattle, the previous

December. It was clear that my message intended to hold their feet to the fire while challenging them to rise and fight as they had in the opening tournament. However, a deafening quiet met this brilliant speech. Then, after what seemed like a lifetime, one of the players spoke up and said, "Coach, we think the problem is you don't have any faith in us!"

Bear in mind the greatest percentage of coaches I know would take such a comment as heresy and lash back at the author of such diatribe. But my manner is to respond to any personal attack with silence while I ask myself if it is true. During the stillness, I put my hands palms down on the edge of the stage, leaned forward and stared at the floor for what seemed a long while. I asked myself if it were true.

I rose up, squinted at them in the dim light, and said, "You're absolutely right!"

This gained their attention, and I continued. "Even though I don't believe in the star system, I confess that after the last two games, I said to myself, without Peter, we might not score another goal all season."

I then added, "If you will forgive me, I will renew my pledge that the Smurfs can do together what Peter might have been able to do on his own."

I dismissed them to get ready for practice, which would be a 30-minute drive to Barry University. At that time, the Barry coach was my former Seattle Pacific player Sergio, who we would play the next day before heading to Chicago for the Wheaton College Invitational. I then left the ballroom and headed for the penthouse level (preferring the highest floor in hotels where I stay.)

Shortly there was a knock on my door, which I approached thinking it might be the player who accused me in the meeting. I should have known it would be John Richardson, my assistant coach, and goalkeeper in our 1985 championship against FIU. John was then, and always has been, one of my closest friends. He is the most honest and blunt individual. We can say anything to each other and usually do. John's message was clear.

"Now that you have cleared the air," he said, "you need to bring to practice something wild, crazy and new to show everybody we are not going to do the same old stuff."

I thanked him for the insight and sat down at my desk to preview what I had planned for that day and where I might introduce something new.

VOILA! One of the drills I designed was a five-man shooting exercise that began at the halfway stripe and ended with a realistic shot on goal. After a few repetitions, I added defenders to make it more game-like. Regrettably, many of these forays ended with an errant cross from the flanks (wing area of the field). This resulted in five players simply sprinting 60 yards only to experience frustration, usually aimed at a teammate who failed to cross the ball properly. The more I stared at the diagram – and departure time for Barry– I asked myself, what if we kept the same drill but moved everybody 40 yards closer to the goal? In short, why not compress the drill and put the whole team around the penalty area? BINGO!

It would take 47 tombs of how to coach soccer to explain how successful and enjoyable the drill has been. And, true to what I share with coaches and players, it's always good to give a drill a name so time is not wasted explaining it. Since the drill was born in the Bahia Mar Hotel in Florida, the drill is called BAHIA!

The next day we shellacked Barry U, winning 5-0. Then we headed on to Chicago for two more victories. Back in Seattle, two months later, the Smurfs, led by twin dynamo co-captains Mark Faller and Danny Machado, won another national championship. At the time, the Falcons were the first ever team to win back-to-back national soccer championships in NCAA history. And, oh, by the way, the final score was 4-1. We had the largest scoring margin in championship play to that time!

Chapter 42
Joe Bean

Winning Strategy:
Master a meaningful handshake.

I have carried with me an insight learned from street fights in my youth.

When duking it out, often I would catch a glimpse of a twinkle in my

opponent's eye. Intuitively, I knew that twinkle would lead to some sort of

alliance, perhaps even a friendship once the blood stopped flowing.

Early in my career as a soccer coach, that insight certainly was the case

with Joe Bean, a future Hall of Fame coach I first met as an adversary, who

has since become one of my best friends on the planet. Joe was the head soccer

coach of Quinnipiac College in Hamden, Connecticut. This meant his team

was the opponent we, the Gordon College Fighting Scots of Wenham,

Massachusetts, would face in the regional final of the NAIA (National

Association of Intercollegiate Athletics) national championships in 1964.

The NAIA ruled that teams vying for the finals should play the deciding games at neutral sites. That site for our game was at Nichols College in Dudley, Massachusetts, approximately half way between the North Shore of Boston and Hamden. It was about an hour and a half drive for each team. We journeyed to Nichols and once there, host personnel directed us to a dressing room in the athletic field house. I tidied up my pre-game speech with the team and, as was my custom, sought solace for myself for similar, personal preparation.

The Quinnipiac team arrived first, assigned the women's dressing room on the opposite side of the field house from my team, but I was unaware of that. There was a centrally located restroom at the midway that was a common bathroom for anyone in the adjoining dressing area. Thus, I entered the restroom at the same second Joe Bean entered the restroom from his side.

Coach Bean wore slacks, sport coat, white shirt and tie, and held a clipboard tucked under one arm. He stuck out his hand and said, "Hi, I'm Joe Bean, head coach of Quinnipiac. I did likewise and said, "I'm Cliff McCrath, from Gordon."

At that instant, three things flashed through my mind: One, I knew he was a Christian; two, I knew we would be friends for life, and, three, I knew we were going to beat them! All three proved to be true.

Like me, Joe was an All American Athlete in soccer, but he has me beat since he was also an All American in baseball. Years after this first meeting, I recruited him as one of the coaches for an all-star soccer goodwill trip for the U.S. State Department in Central and South America. Joe didn't speak Spanish, but accepted the moniker *"Jose Frijoles"* when we told him it was a name of distinction. Even though he eventually discovered it translated Joe Beans he graciously accepted it, and to his loving friends he is still Jose Frijoles.

One slight departure from that occurred when I keynoted his 2007 retirement party in Wheaton College's auditorium. He served as Wheaton's head soccer coach from 1969-2006. During the event, the school officials announced they were going to name the soccer field after him. That night, in my speech, I pointed out how great it was to be the only university in the country to play soccer in a Bean Field! Within days, the school renamed it Joe Bean Stadium.

Wheaton's Joe Bean aka Jose Frijoles is one of my closest friends on the planet. He is a graduate of East Stroudsburg College in Pennsylvania and married to Shirley ("The Perl"). Joe is therefore a fanatical fan of the Philadelphia Phillies, whereas I am a Detroit Tigers fan (another book required on that). Joe and Shirley have four children, two girls and two boys. All are happily married and all but one (a pastor) live within five miles of them. I stay with them four to five times a year in Wheaton near Old Lawson Field, where I first saw a soccer ball in the fall of 1955.

At his retirement banquet, we got a good laugh over the only time Joe ever displayed overt frustration. It occurred during halftime of a game that featured the worst display of soccer a Bean team had ever delivered. For some reason, Joe remained on the field contrary to the halftime ritual when coach and players review and adjust for the second half of the game, usually in the locker room. Time wore on, and still no Joe.

The team knew how badly they had played and wondered if Joe, indeed, would even show up. Just about the time the two teams were due back on the field, Joe appeared with a look of consternation on his face. With a clipboard tucked under one arm he halted, stared, then held up one finger in a scolding manner and said, "Boys, one word: NOT GOOD!"

To this day, when facing a mishap or difficult situation, his sons and I still use the patent expression, "One word. Not Good!"

Joe began his coaching career at Quinnipiac, which at the time was an NAIA school (small college), but after great success he was offered a post at the NCAA Division II school Bridgeport University in Connecticut. Then, based on Joe's acceptance, the school was upgraded to Division I.

Incidentally, Seattle Pacific played Bridgeport in the 1986 national semifinal when my son Steve was a freshman at SPU, (he started the play that led to the go-ahead goal). The game ended in a 2-1 victory for us. In the next game, we defeated Oakland, Michigan, 4-1, for the largest margin of victory to date in NCAA collegiate soccer playoffs.

The Bridgeport (retiring) coach at that time (1986) was a longtime friend of mine named Fran Bacon whose dream it was to exit a champion. I was quoted in the paper as saying to my team, "Fran is my dear friend, but let him drink milk after this game and figure out when and where he would like to drink champagne at another time!"

Meanwhile, double back to Wheaton and Joe Bean. When Coach B., Dr. Robert Baptista, took the college presidency at Sterling College in Kansas, he offered the coaching position he would vacate at Wheaton to me. It was a great honor, but I had just signed to coach at Seattle Pacific (beginning in 1970).

"However," I said, "I have the perfect guy for you! Joe Bean." This was in late December, just weeks before the annual coach's convention in New York. I corralled Joe and led him to Coach B., made the introductions and left the two of them alone. During that time together, Joe made clear he would not break the contract to coach Bridgeport, though it would be a dream to coach at Wheaton. He made such an impression that Coach B. sealed the deal and employed an interim coach, (Russ Enlow) until Joe could take over the following year.

Joe retired after the 2006 season after setting a new national collegiate soccer record of 66 consecutive games without a defeat and the NCAA record of 607 collegiate wins (to my 597). Thus, at his retirement, he was the top winning soccer coach in NCAA Division II history, and I was number two.

At his retirement banquet, he pointed down to me from the lectern in his remarks (after my keynote speech), saying, "But this man will break my record this coming season!"

Little did he know Seattle Pacific would win only seven games that season and on November 2, 2007, after 49 years of coaching, 38 at Seattle, my time as head coach would abruptly come to an end. This meant I did not break my good friend's record.

Chapter 43
Letting Go

Winning Strategy:
Even a loss can be a win.

Victories, oh yes, I've had some great victories, but there are no pithy phrases for despair, which is sometimes an outright mental battle.

Even winning teams may experience a great amount of discord. The overriding principle one likes to believe is that the team is a big happy family and the coach is the head of the family. However, there have been teams who have hated each other (see the Oakland A's in the 1970's), yet accomplished great things.

There is the notion, I've come to believe, that even a loss can be a win. It may be the loss of a game, a job, or it may be a loss or failure of another type. For instance, I think I have at times failed– by word or actions – to convey my love.

Earlier in my life, I did not share how deeply hurt I was by divorce. After the divorce from Midge, I turned to Mama B. for counsel, (Martha Baptista, Coach B.'s wife). At Wheaton, after my freshman year, there were seven athletes (including me) living in the Baptista's home as there were not enough dorms on campus at the time. There were three bedrooms for us to share, and one tiny eave bedroom.

After the divorce from Midge, I thought I had sinned. I had not provided focus. I had not gone to find help. We were going down the wrong path. I confessed my guilt over that to Mama B.

She immediately said, "Well that's what forgiveness is all about." Since then, I've said those words to other people experiencing guilt.

Although Midge and I had the most beautiful divorce in the history of divorces, I thought I'd never smile again when it was over.

Midge and I began the journey at Seattle Pacific together, but in 2007 when I was let go by the school, I was alone.

How does one learn to stay strong in times of adversity, through extreme emotional pain and setbacks? It helps to remember that losses are precious life lessons in our spiritual development.

"For everything you have missed, you have gained something else;

and for everything you gain, you lose something else."

~Ralph Waldo Emerson, 1803-1882.

Chapter 44
The Most Beautiful Game Ever Played

Winning Strategy:
When you have nothing to lose, go for broke.

When a team is down two goals or more with little time left, there is no choice, but refuse to lose. (See American basketball coach John Calipari.) The strategy at this point is to go for broke, and risk everything in an all-out effort. When losing badly, the team should play like there's no tomorrow and have nothing left at the end of the game.

I was coaching the Falcons in a semi-final game against FIT when we were behind 5-3 and the clock was running out. There appeared to be little to no chance left of winning. With a bit more discipline, we would not have been in that dire position, but found ourselves forced to play without our main goalkeeper due to a red card in the previous game.

In the prior game, we faced Sonoma State University from California coached by Marcus Ziemer ("Batman") to this day one of my closest friends and a curator of fine wines. My half time speech focused on marking the Sonoma left winger, who was very fast. "Keep your discipline," I cautioned.

Unfortunately, the opposite happened. With eight minutes to go in that game, the Sonoma winger from Asia was flying down the field. I looked, but our goalkeeper Marcus was not in the goal. Where was he?

Marcus was an All-American Athlete, who played the goalkeeper position with skill and control, letting very few goals get by him. Yet, at that moment, he was 40 yards up the field and far outside the goal box when the Sonoma winger made a fast break for the goal. Perhaps his instinct to block all goals triggered him to tackle the Sonoma winger from behind. However, this foul on the opposing team player denied a goal-scoring opportunity.

"Unfortunately," the ref said, "you know I have to eject Marcus."

I said, "I know, I wrote the rule."

Our goalkeeper was kicked out of that game and the next one. Thus, we faced Florida without our main keeper and we were behind near the end of the match. It didn't look good for us.

What gave us the strength to win? Was it the "let's go crazy" factor, or was it training? This game has since been dubbed, "the greatest game of football ever played" by an English sportswriter who had traveled to see many of his countrymen play the game. (FIT also had a Leigh-on-Sea player, Richard Sharpe, who still holds the all-time collegiate scoring record – 148 goals – and holds the NCAA record for assists in a championship game – five – registered in our historic game.)

When a team comes from behind to win, it feels astounding. And when it looks like a certain loss, the win feels even better. What determines success? Studies of winning international football teams find the learning curve is correlated to playing more top-level games. Another common element is team spirit. After more than two decades as head coach of the Falcons, we had perhaps more national championship experience than any other team and a rousing team spirit to match.

In a review of 1,500 important international matches since 1960, final minute goal scoring occurred in just four percent of the games, yet the Dutch and German teams score in the final minute 37 to 47 percent more often (5.5 percent and 5.9 percent of the time, respectively). Is there anything unusual to learn from their styles?

The "Total Football" of the Dutch is the cerebral and controlled style of keeping the ball as much as possible (popular for decades, though it fell out of favor in recent years). In opposition to this technique, the German team developed a high-pressure defensive style called gegenpressing, which translates loosely "counter press."

"Shrinking the field," which I train my teams to do, is the Pacific Northwest version of "Welcome to the Gegenpress." In 1993, the year of our "most beautiful game ever played," *gegenpress* wasn't the buzzword it later became, so I didn't use the term with my teams. However, the concept is similar. What it means is that players re-take and keep possession higher up the field, closer to the opponent's goal, and the defensive line stays high (a key feature of gegenpressing) to frustrate the opposition and force mistakes and turnovers.

(Incidentally, the Spanish and Italians are known for pressing, too, in a variety of formats, including full pressing, partial pressing and fake pressing, wherein they pretend to press, but are really recuperating.)

Applying high pressure in the final minutes of a game is a straightforward strategy. The team applies full pressing ("goes for broke") to force turnovers and keep the ball near the goal for scoring opportunities. High pressure defending causes the other team to make mistakes. (A team's fitness, discipline and endurance must be superior, due to everyday training – stamina is key.) The team then rapidly exploits the vulnerability of lost possession while still in the other teams' defensive zone. Once again on offense, with the playing field minimized to the final 30 yards of the field, scoring opportunities are higher and come more quickly.

In sum, when losing and the clock is running out, shrinking the field frustrates the opposing team and forces mistakes and turnovers. When in a winning position, with two minutes or less left in the game, shrinking the field and controlling the ball also protects the lead.

Does it work? Yes. Hence the quote:

"Football is a simple game; 22 men chase a ball for 90 minutes and at the end, the Germans win." ~ Gary Lineker, BBC Sport presenter and former England captain.

Chapter 45
Teachable Moments

Winning Strategy:
Happiness lies in the joy of overcoming.

Challenged by my college roommate in 1955 to turn out for soccer, I scoffed thinking it was a playground activity for girls. To come to the point, it was in my mind that the battle to accept his challenge was won. Four days after joining the team, we played our first game, and there was no turning back for me. By my third year, I was an Honorable Mention All American in the sport. The next year, I was the team coach. Since then, winning games against superior teams has been the hallmark of the entire journey.

Perhaps, the greatest example of how my mind won supremacy over obstacles was figuring out how to survive being fired as head coach of soccer at Seattle Pacific, after a lifetime of love. This included more than 500 wins, multiple conference championships, 30 postseason NCAA playoffs, 15 Final

Fours and 10 national finals, of which we won five. Yet, the years of devotion that began with moving my young family to Seattle in 1970 ended with two words from the athletic director, "It's time."

Part of overcoming such a traumatic setback came via a flashback. Decades earlier, I was invited by this school to become dean of students and coach a fledging soccer program that had won just a single game in its first two years (1968-69). After many triumphs, it would not be right to sum up the entire experience based on the final moment.

It was not always easy. My career has been the crucible where I was able to hone the moral imperatives that guide my every step! Peel me to the bone and I'll head for Ethiopia or the back alleys of the world to help kids get to a higher road today. That's my ideal coaching job now. (Sure, I'd also love to be a hockey and/or baseball announcer at the major league level!)

When I decided to accept God's will for me, once I made the decision to do it, enthusiasm fueled the dream and helped me to do the work. I have no plans to rest on my laurels. I'm very enthusiastic about Northwest Soccer Camp (in 2018, we just finished our 47th year) and a new project of great merit, "Hand in Hand." This is a free soccer camp and non-profit youth soccer program (created by Todd McNeal, a parent, and Gordon Lacey a successful businessman with vision and a love for kids) helping underprivileged youth in Everett, Washington. I'm proud to be a part of that.

Growing a successful program from the grass roots up is very challenging, but I'm reminded of the wise words of my early mentor, Coach B. My Wheaton soccer coach went on to become president of two universities and by his very existence inspired hundreds of players. He shared his definition of success in one of his inaugural addresses as university president: "Of what significance is the victory if the challenge is too small!"

Happiness lies in the "happenings" of life to be sure and achievement is one of the most satisfying ways to experience pure joy. But there is another type of sweet victory, and that is the joy of overcoming a difficult obstacle. This opportunity often comes disguised in a teachable moment.

Dr. Kenneth Foreman, my farting buddy and, at once, my advocate, tutor and, occasional adversary, was 96 when he died on December 23, 2018. He was the former head coach of the US Olympic track team and is a Hall of Fame member of the US Track and Field Association.

Three teachable moments from my longtime friend come to mind.

One, in the throes of a Miami heat wave my Seattle Falcons team lost a game to my son's Barry University team, (on fire as a young coach) after which I ordered my team to line up and run sprints for what I had determined was an inferior performance.

Foreman and his wife Denise travelled there to cheer for both teams. (She holds three world records in Master's Track and Field, was an All-American hurdler in college and a member of the U.S. Track & Field team.) They leaned over the fence while my team was laboring through the sprints and I ambled over to where they were standing. "What do you think?" I asked.

In true Bev Jacques mode he said, "Well, if you're goal is to punish them, you're succeeding!" POW!

Another teachable moment for me came when I studied his tutoring of his Olympic athlete Kelly Blair LaBounty practicing the long jump. This event requires the approaching athlete to leave the ground in a thrusting manner common to jumping off a grounded starting point. I watched, amazed – make that mesmerized – as he said, "When you leave the ground and are at the peak of your lift your thigh needs to be parallel to the ground!" POW. Double POW. POWWOW! In all my coaching tips, I NEVER was that finite in tutoring a player. It would be kind of like telling one of my soccer players he would be a better goal scorer if he tied his shoes with the knots an inch closer to his heel!

A third gem was when I was about to depart to coach the U.S. Women's World University Games team having never coached women in such high-level competition. Ken, Denise ("Nisi"), and I lived together in Seattle and Hawaii for more 20 years, so I sauntered over to his easy chair and asked him, "Any tips you can give me before we leave for Taiwan?"

He said, "Coach them like men!" (Three months later, he celebrated his 95th birthday and we defeated four of the world's most powerful women's teams: South Korea, Taiwan, Mexico and Argentina.

Another one of my most treasured tutor-mentors – and best friend on the planet - is one of my former players. Paul MacVittie (now Harvard-educated Dr. Paul MacVittie), was an athletes on my team at Gordon College in Wenham, Massachusetts, the first year soccer replaced football at the school. As a senior in college and triple-sport athlete (an all-star in all three: football, basketball and baseball), he turned out for the first-ever soccer team that I was to coach.

We were both products of the streets – me from Detroit and he from Bridgeport, Connecticut. We were close in age but he was/is miles ahead in worldly wisdom. His wise counsel and insights would fill an encyclopedia of life's nuggets, for not only survival but also robust daily living.

I gave him his first lessons in golf (circa 1960-something) when I needed another golfer for a tournament foursome. We hit a few balls into the swamp behind my house---a dormitory at Gordon College.

Fifty-two years later, I visited him at his golf club in the bowels of a New Hampshire forest, playing a few holes before postgame libations. Lined up on a back-nine tee box, I became frustrated with my tee shots, which with grievous consistency, landed in nearby arbors of pine trees and adjacent bodies of water.

In a quiet, unobtrusive, unsolicited mode, he stood to my rear, right side, and calmly said, "One o'clock!"

I stopped and stared, and inquired, "One o'clock?"

He said, "Aim for one o'clock!"

That was years ago and from that next swing to this, my drives are straight down the pike!

Chapter 46
Ike D.

Winning Strategy:
Choose to play.

A personal example of choosing attitude over insurmountable odds comes from the time I was team-teaching a roomful of professionals taking part in a degree completion program for City University.

The tag team of profs included an NBA basketball coach, a former Olympic Track and Field coach (Foreman), and me. The basketball coach spoke of the unique aspects of smaller NBA players who, somehow, were able to compete in an industry featuring giants. The track coach, a physiologist, attributed excellence in achievement to genetics and fast twitch muscles.

I, on the other hand, addressed the issue of effort and heart as a key ingredient in achievement. At the end of the formal presentations, there was a Question and Answer session during which it was obvious my philosophy would be under considerable scrutiny. The debate between effort, heart and talent became a bit heated, the climax, of which, was my pal Foreman, the track coach, emphatically stating, "McCrath, if I had a million dollars, I couldn't get a one-legged man to jump seven feet!"

Obviously, when up against such odds (such as significant Olympic-level physiology expertise), the tendency is to withdraw and figuratively cower in a corner. Nonetheless, it was at that very moment I came to, realizing my whole life had been battling against the "givens" (i.e. so-called facts of life).

I said, without malice, "I don't care if he doesn't jump seven feet, I just want him to jump!"

There are thousands of quotes amplifying the principle of attitude over all odds. One of my favorites is by the author Mark Twain. He wrote, "It's not the size of the dog in the fight; it's the size of the fight in the dog!"

Attitude and effort are essential for lasting success. Success that lasts is its own press secretary providing the talking points that highlight what works. Just as all motivation comes from external stimuli, success comes from arriving at a predestined plateau or the exceptional effort to get there.

Not everyone is as preoccupied with winning as the only description of success. Special Olympics participants, for example, hold a more elevated definition of success, perhaps, than others would. I discovered this when attending a ceremony at the Washington State governor's mansion honoring members of the Washington State Special Olympics Team. A young man with two artificial legs approached the mic and humbly said, "I so desperately want to win, but if I can't, may I be noble in the attempt."

By contrast, other people have a self-image that is so low that no amount of success – as the world sees it – convinces them that they are OK. There are legions framed to believe that regardless of how well they have done, it is not good enough. These people need to know that no matter how insignificant they feel every life may have an impact on others in a positive way.

By way of example, more than 2.7 million people watched the YouTube video of an act of compassion in my neck of the woods. It occurred in 2010 in Snohomish, a small town about 30 miles northeast of Seattle. A 16-year-old with Down syndrome, Ike played on the school's junior varsity football team. His coaches ended each practice with a play they called the "Ike Special," in which Ike took a handoff from the fullback and ran all the way to the end zone to score a touchdown. Though Ike scored a touchdown in each practice, he never got to play in a game. That is, until September 24, 2010. Ike entered the home game against Lake Stevens High School on the last play. Everyone in Snohomish's home stadium knew the team was going to run the "Ike Special." The opponents knew it, too. And, in the video that went viral, Ike, #57 outruns all the defenders who dive and miss him during his 51-yard run to victory. It is an amazing experience to see the beauty of it. Though years from now no one is likely to remember who won the game or what the score was, the people who were there and the people who saw the video will not forget Ike's moment of glory.

Choose to play, and be noble in the attempt.

Chapter 47
Action!

Winning Strategy:
Always have something exciting going for yourself.

Home again in Seattle, I watch the sun breaking brightly around the clouds over Lake Union. With a cup of coffee in hand, I watch a crew team stroke swiftly in unison, the silvery sun reflected across the water.

I think Malachi 4:2 best sums up what I pray my Lord and Savior Jesus Christ wants me to live out the rest of my days on the planet: "But for you who revere my name, the sun of righteousness will rise with healing in his wings. And you will go free, leaping with joy like calves released from the stall!"

What I hope is that when people close this book, there is a feeling of movement and the desire to take action. For those in a rut, a change in habits is needed, because habits drain the juice from life. Altering habits (or just breaking away from the routine) changes thinking. Although there is nothing wrong with hard work, working harder without getting results is a form of failure, and a wake-up call to do things differently.

There is a simple method useful to leap out of the rut. Tomorrow morning get out of bed in a new way. Drink a glass of water and take a cold shower. (See world famous photographer Chase Jarvis) Then, keep a journal all day and record what was different. This costs nothing but takes a conscious act of the will. No philosophical inspiration is required to try it.

The habit of language should also be contemplated. There may be times, when a coach feels it necessary to say to a player, "Get your ass out there and do what I think you should do." Other times, there may be no alternative but to hand down, "OK, now we're going to do it my way." That said, a change of language, choosing to speak excellently, alters the trajectory of outcomes rather quickly and dramatically when put into practice. Another aspect of language to evaluate is self-talk. Great coaches, and great achievers, never accept themselves as ordinary. They become something extraordinary.

This leads me to my final words of wisdom and the 47th winning strategy, "Always have something exciting going for you!"

Here are some final ideas for how to begin:

Volunteer to coach a youth sports team, learn something new, go to a sporting event and cheer, host a party, have an adventure, do a random act of kindness and take an interest in people.

It took me 40 years to discover my gift as an Itinerant Edifier. Great achievers never give up. They never accept society's definition of what can and cannot be done, and they put the needs of others above those of their own.

List of Acronyms and Abbreviations

AFL: American Football League

AGC: Associated General Contractors

Alabama A&M: Alabama Agricultural and Mechanical University

CA: Critical Assumptions

Coach B.:   Dr. Robert Baptista

FIU: Florida International University

Ike D.:   Ike Ditzenberger

Mama B.:   Martha Baptista (wife of Dr. Robert Baptista)

NAIA: National Association of Intercollegiate Athletics

NASL: National American Soccer League

NBA: National Basketball Association

NCAA: National Collegiate Athletic Association

NFL: National Football League

PDA: Personal Death Awareness

SPC/SPU: Seattle Pacific College; Seattle Pacific University

UCLA: University of California Los Angeles

USC: University of Southern California

UW: University of Washington

37778121R10142

Made in the USA
Middletown, DE
02 March 2019